When We Worked Hard

TICKLE COVE, NEWFOUNDLAND

When We Worked Hard
TICKLE COVE, NEWFOUNDLAND

DARRELL DUKE

Flanker Press Ltd.
St. John's, NL

Library and Archives Canada Cataloguing in Publication

Duke, Darrell, 1970–

　　When we worked hard : a history of Tickle Cove, Newfoundland / Darrell Duke.

Includes index.

ISBN 978-1-897317-04-4

　　1. Tickle Cove (N.L.)--History.　2. Tickle Cove (N.L.)--Biography.　I. Title.

FC2199.T52D83 2007　　　　　　971.8　　　　　　C2007-900309-5

PRINTED IN CANADA

FLANKER PRESS
P.O. BOX 2522, STATION C
ST. JOHN'S, NL, CANADA A1C 6K1
TOLL FREE: 1-866-739-4420
WWW.FLANKERPRESS.COM

First Canadian edition printed May 2007

11 10 09 08 07　　　　　1 2 3 4 5 6

We acknowledge the financial support of: the Government of Canada through the Book Publishing Industry Development Program (BPIDP); the Canada Council for the Arts which last year invested $20.1 million in writing and publishing throughout Canada; the Government of Newfoundland and Labrador, Department of Tourism, Culture and Recreation.

The research phase of this project was funded by Human Resources and Development Canada.

In Memory of

Margaret Houlihan (1912–2004)
Bernadette Murray (1916–2004)
Mary McCue (1928–2004)
Cyril O'Reilly (1937–2004)

To my dear friend, Captain John Russell, for his boundless
giving of time, memories, laughter, and tears.

Contents

NEWFOUNDLAND

Bonavista

Tickle Cove

Clarenville

St. John's

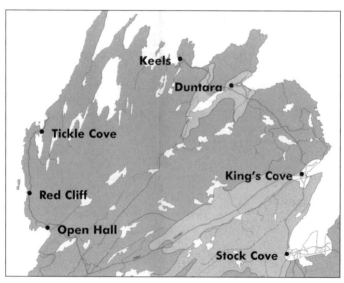

Keels

Duntara

Tickle Cove

King's Cove

Red Cliff

Open Hall

Stock Cove

Foreword

TICKLE COVE AT first glance revealed only rock. Gracefully, beaches with stories to tell appeared. Old houses, once homes, were strewn about the landscape.

To the left, across a small beach, a collaboration of wind and whitecaps echoed of distant fiddles, the sounds rising and falling with each gentle swell of the ocean.

Resting peacefully to the right was Tickle Cove Pond, the only part of the town I'd ever heard of in song. Written more than a century ago by a native of the town, I'd often heard *"Tickle Cove Pond"* sung by old folks. It always left me sad with a longing to find the pond, stand at its edge, and imagine the narrator's plight. Now here I was, but little did I know Kit's near-death experience would pale with other stories of the quiet little town.

After driving as far as the road would allow, I walked along a well-beaten path and marvelled over the majestic sea and the increasing serenity brought on by the summer's fragrances.

From their grassy blankets, retired fishing nets gasped for one last taste of salt water and the security of tired hands in search of the next meal. Once-sturdy fences, cut without the aid of modernization, crept back into the ground from which they came.

Appearing as natural as the sloped meadow which houses them, two old cemeteries provided the first insight into the names of people who once shared this cove. Rockpiles indicated hard preparation for growing vegetables. The musical winds which had faded in the distance returned as if inviting me back to see more.

The left side of Tickle Cove harbour exposed a row of rusty yet dignified grapnels adjacent to the town's only remaining fish stage. In the shelter of more rock, remnants of an old dwelling lay in a pile waiting to be burned in a once-typical beachside fire. An easy aura accompanied my every step throughout this, what now seemed to be a familiar community.

How exciting I thought it would be to have the privilege of digging up the past of these houses, coves, meadows, and waters. As fate should have it, by summer's end I was making my way over "The Big Hill" to speak with Mike and Marge O'Shea, one of many seasonal families who call Tickle Cove home. They have been coming here for over thirty-seven years and fondly recall the gentle welcome by the community's people.

When inquiring of what was okay to do, and where was okay to go, the O'Sheas were always met with the response, "Whatever pleases you, me son." This open gesture, first bestowed upon the New York couple by Mr. O'Shea's uncle, the late Samuel Legge, clearly depicts the laid-back demeanour of the people.

Although it continues to feel the gruelling effects of government's resettlement plan for rural Newfoundland, Tickle Cove has been able to savour what's left of "the way it was." Trust, a key component in keeping relationships strong, is evident in the way residents still rely on the "tick," or credit, at the town's sole convenience store.

Several remarkable Tickle Cove people played vital roles in the history of Newfoundland and Labrador. Days gone by are recalled by those who gambled for survival against an unforgiving land and sea.

Due to the small number of citizens with a solid memory of yesteryear, it is impossible to give a full-fledged account of every Tickle Cove family and community event.

A handful of resourceful individuals provide the contents of this book which mostly deal with the latter portion of the 1800s and the first half of the 1900s. Either from legend or personal experience, information is presented as it would in rural conversation.

Following the ways of their forefathers, folks did without so others would not. A resilient crowd indeed, the people of Tickle Cove have seen a great deal and continue to survive through change.

Without need for exaggeration or skepticism, by the book's end I am certain Tickle Cove will find a warranted place in your heart.

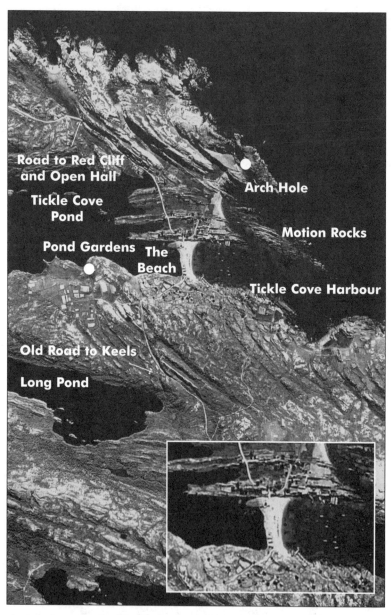

Aerial photograph of Tickle Cove taken in 1951. Insert shows a magnified view of Tickle Cove. (Courtesy of Government of Newfoundland and Labrador, Surveys and Mapping Division.)

About Tickle Cove

The people of Tickle Cove worked hard.

Rita Tremblett

THE BONAVISTA PENINSULA, located on the eastern side of the island of Newfoundland, consists of Trinity Bay North on one side and Bonavista Bay South on the other. Tickle Cove is a small community located on the south side of Bonavista Bay. The valley-like settlement is fifty-one kilometres southwest of historic Bonavista, seventy-four kilometres northeast of the island's east coast hub, Clarenville, and 260 kilometres north of St. John's, the capital of the province of Newfoundland and Labrador.

First-time visitors to Tickle Cove may wonder why people chose to settle in such isolation two centuries ago. There *is* no mystery. They went there to fish. Before roads connected Newfoundland's communities, the sea was the highway and boats were the standard form of transporta-

1

tion and communication. The closeness of villages like Tickle Cove to the fishing grounds was certainly a plus. Not that life was easy, by any stretch of the imagination.

Also included in a three-kilometre span of oceanfront properties, spongy meadows, and rock are the settlements of Red Cliff and Open Hall. The three communities have shared more than two centuries of life and death against long, cold winters and short Newfoundland summers.

To the northeast of Tickle Cove are the communities of Keels and Duntarra. Both personal and work-related interactions between the three settlements were forged by what has long been called "The Old Road to Keels." This inland route for trading, setting slips, cutting wood, and picking berries was more easily travelled during winter months over ice and snow.

Other nearby settlements of Bonavista Bay South include Plate Cove East, Plate Cove West, Stock Cove, Knight's Cove, Sommerville (formerly Indian Arm), Princeton (formerly Seal Cove), Southern Bay, and Sweet Bay. Each of these communities played a vital role in both the economic and social relations of Tickle Cove. In fact, many of these places were settled by folks from once-over-crowded centres including Tickle Cove, King's Cove, and Bonavista.

Tickle Cove's coastline is defined by lines of protruding rocks known as *tickles*. Seafarers must use careful navigation to manoeuvre successfully around these dangerous outcroppings. Tickles provide shelter for small craft and are situated fairly close to the fishing grounds. In the centre of the town lies a beach, long used for all realms of the fishery, which separates the ocean harbour from Tickle Cove Pond.

Although it played a crucial role in the lives of Tickle Cove's people, the beach lay in the hands of a merciless sea. The relatively shallow harbour, combined with soaring winds and high tides, are perfect ingredients for severe inshore currents and destructive waves.

UNDERSTANDING HISTORY

An understanding of conditions in Ireland prior to and during the arrival of Irish immigrants to Newfoundland is essential to explaining the values and ethics of our forefathers, in particular the calm demeanour in the personalities of Tickle Cove people.

Since the first invasion of Ireland by the English in 1169, Ireland's land has been confiscated and redistributed countless times. In 1798, with the aid of France, the Irish rebelled. Despite its army of 100,000 men, Ireland remained under the control of England. On January 1, 1801, the Act of Union between Ireland and England became operative. Both countries were made one.

Free trade between the two indicated the discrimination practiced by England against Irish industry would come to an end. The reality of the situation, however, proved quite differently. The new Act, bitterly opposed, was seen not as a marriage. In Smith's *The Great Hunger*, Ireland was compared to an heiress whose "chambermaid and trustees had been bribed, while she herself is dragged kicking and screaming to the altar."

Although records indicate a major influx of Irish to Newfoundland between the late 1700s and the mid 1800s, Ireland incredibly maintained a 172 per cent increase in its population, a sure natural aid in the spread of famine and disease.

Unlike its centuries-old conqueror, Ireland did not become industrialized. Its deposits of coal and iron attracted more geologists than economists. By 1845, the few industries it did possess wobbled on their last legs. The Irish spoke of "famine fever," but, in fact, two separate diseases were present: typhus fever and relapsing fever, both carried by the common louse. It would be nearly sixty years following the "Black Year" of 1847 before the nature of the scourge was understood.

It is unknown, exactly, how many thousands died as a result of the famine and the fever in Ireland, but approximately 1,250,000 Irish are said to have migrated to the shores of North America during this time.

The fisheries of Ireland too, were underdeveloped. For example, in Galway and Mayo herring fishermen were too poor to purchase salt to preserve their catches.

When it came to agriculture, unless an Irish labourer could secure a piece of land and grow potatoes to feed himself and his family, they starved. Families often divided small portions of land to be used between several generations of a family. This practice of sparing land and its contents was carried on in Tickle Cove for generations. For example, brothers Jim and Andrew Maloney shared a garden where both families sowed their own vegetables.

In Ireland, it was not compulsory to register births until 1863, and though the practice of taking a census every ten years began in 1821, the first figures considered reliable are those of 1841. As for determining the first settlers in Tickle Cove, literature is scarce. Keels is identified on a map as early as 1582, and served as an English fishing station by 1675. Other sources showing an English settlement at Keels in 1702 may indicate, due to its reasonable closeness, at least seasonal work activities took place at Tickle Cove around that time. However, no strong supporting evidence exists. In addition to being well-situated for a small boat fishery, Tickle Cove had the advantage of a substantial hinterland for winter work in the southern arms of Bonavista Bay.

Why did people settle in Tickle Cove? There was no privileged class in Newfoundland which meant early settlers could hunt and fish wherever and whenever they pleased. Ireland was heavily taxed by both church and state. They were used to no political freedom. Not even the right to vote. Unlike in their homeland, Irish settlers in Newfoundland did not have to rival with despised English landlords. Land at places such as Tickle Cove was free and plentiful for the growing of root crops, and to provide hay for cattle. Timber for fuel, boats, houses, stages, flakes, and fences was in abundance. Meat was constantly supplied by a variety of wild birds and animals.

Natives of England equally helped settle Tickle Cove. It is likely Tickle Cove was also an outpost for settlers of Salvage, located at the tip of the Eastport Peninsula, one of the earliest harbours to be employed by migratory fishermen from England. Like many Newfoundland outports, Tickle Cove was a desirable location for English fishers choosing to flee from the inconsistencies of their seasonal occupation. Tired of travelling across the Atlantic Ocean on the empty promises of greedy merchants, a new start seemed more appealing. Although the British Admiralty searched for deserters, dangerous tickles protecting the hazardous shoreline were difficult to navigate. If caught, defectors were punished by hanging from the ship's yardarm.

The English and the French had been battling over fishing rights in Newfoundland for 200 years by this time. However, with the Treaty of Utrecht in 1713, the French were forced to settle on northern and western portions of the colony, as well as the islands of St. Pierre et Miquelon. The English claimed rights to the rest of the territory.

Luckily for the inhabitants of Bonavista Bay, the English focused the brunt of their attention on the Avalon Peninsula. This allowed the former, at least, some freedom to live as they pleased. With securing a livelihood far ahead of the need for social status, rural folk were not as involved in religious and racial bigotry as a means of determining where they belonged. Unfortunately, the same could not be said of the upper classes of St. John's, where religion fuelled centuries of

12

foolishness, the instigators being church authorities and political figures. This is not to say there were no exceptions in the outports.

Records indicate the surname Mullowney had connections to Tickle Cove in the late 1700s. William Mullowney, born *circa* 1750 near Sligo, Ireland, sailed to Newfoundland around 1775 on the ship *The Irish Maid*. It was on this voyage Mullowney's wife gave birth to a son, William.

It is likely the Mullowneys settled in or near Bonavista due to the active fishery there. They later moved to Tickle Cove to escape overcrowded waters and beaches.

Early in the nineteenth century in Tickle Cove, William, Jr. fathered a son, Andrew. In January 1828, Andrew became the father of Thomas who, as a young man, moved to Sweet Bay. With his first wife, Johanna Kelly, he had one child, Bridget, born *circa* 1850. Johanna died shortly after the birth of their daughter. Bridget Mullowney died at Grand Falls, Newfoundland, in 1927 at age seventy-six.

Thomas married a second time to Catherine O'Neil with whom he had a son, Tom, in 1852. Thomas, Sr. died in Sweet Bay on January 13, 1919, at age ninety.

Another Thomas Mullowney, of Tickle Cove, married an Elizabeth Cullimore in 1816. He died in 1865 at the age of ninety-two. Given the fact he was two years old when William Mullowney and his wife came to Newfoundland from Ireland, it is possible he was their son.

Records indicate a Henry Over occupied a fishing

room on the beach at Tickle Cove in 1806. There is also a John Baker recorded as a settler there in 1810.

The surname Kennedy, long gone from Tickle Cove, has its origins in County Cork, Ireland. In his final years at Tickle Cove, John Kennedy was cared for by a Catherine Kelly and a Mary Kelly, Sr., both of Tickle Cove. Mr. Kennedy, who died *circa* 1838, fished with William Curran of Tickle Cove, another family name no longer affiliated with the town. Mr. Curran, a native of County Waterford, Ireland, married Mary Kelly, Jr. of Tickle Cove in 1829.

A major influx of Irish immigrants to Tickle Cove in the 1820s included the surnames Driscoll, Culleton, Walker, Gorman, Neil, Downey, Walsh, and Connors. In the fifty years to follow, Tickle Cove recorded surnames such as Skiffington, Canning, Roe, Mulcahey (pronounced "Mulky" by locals), Cross, Godfrey, MacCormack, Barker, Lane, Wareham, Greening, Over (or Ovier), White, Powell, Muggeridge, Humby, and Gale. By 1827, Tickle Cove's population stood at 171. The surname Maher is listed there solely for the year 1834.

The population jumped to 247 in 1837. Twenty years later the number of residents at Tickle Cove increased to 356.

Listed as "Pickle Cove" in Hutchinson's 1864–65 directory, Tickle Cove contained one merchant, David J. P. Candow, and three "coopers," or barrel makers, all from the Connors family. The constable at the time, John Skiffington, had also been the town's schoolmaster for roughly thirty years.

By 1871, Tickle Cove's population dropped to 320, perhaps the beginning of a massive out-migration which has continued in varying degrees to the present day. Surnames included Candow, Cross, Dooley, Huxley, Kelly, Lane, Legge, Mullowney (this surname has been changed to and from 'Maloney' several times during the past two centuries), Munchine, Neille, Ovier (or Over), Philpott, Rolls, Russell, Skiffington, Taylor, and White. With the exception of John Taylor, a planter and trader, all men multi-tasked on both land and sea in order to adequately survive.

In 1894, there were 138 fishermen at Tickle Cove and one trader, Archibald C. Candow. With these large numbers, and given the relatively compact harbour of the community, out-migration to nearby settlements seemed inevitable. By 1898, Tickle Cove's population had dropped to 250, then to 205 by 1911. The surname MacCormick disappeared from Tickle Cove around this time. The MacCormicks, like many other families to follow, left to find work in the United States. By this time, Tickle Cove men were leaving the fishery to work for the Anglo-Newfoundland Development Company's (A.N.D.) pulp and paper mill at Grand Falls. By the early 1920s, many men found employment with the Newfoundland Power and Paper Company (later purchased by Bowater Newfoundland Limited) at Corner Brook.

Many families uprooted and moved to the eastern United States, mainly to New York and Massachusetts, while others to the sands of California. They found work as fishermen, fish plant workers, shipbuilders, carpenters, steel workers, and household servants. Rarely could one afford to come home for a visit. Many never returned while others worked for a few years and moved home for good.

Following 1921, Tickle Cove's population of 194 plummeted drastically due to the effects of a tidal surge in the fall of that year. Already shaking up the economy were the strained fish prices, which never fully recovered after the First World War. This, too, added greatly to the demise of the population.

The 1935 census records indicate a population of 120 at Tickle Cove. In 1955 the numbers remained steady at 119. Over the course of the past fifty years, natural selection and out-migration has left Tickle Cove with twenty-seven dwellings and fifty-three residents. Most of the town's senior citizens are seasonal residents, spending winters with family in other areas of the province.

The Kelly brothers of Tickle Cove worked at the A.N.D.'s pulp and paper mill at Grand Falls in the 1920s. L–R: William, Jack, Oswald, Sam, and their stepfather, Edward Bonia. Their brother, Peter, was killed and buried overseas during WWI. (Courtesy of Annie and Mary Kelly)

Tickle Cove's "Arch Hole" has been an attraction for both locals and visitors for generations.

With proper wind and tide, the saltwater surge through the Arch Hole is quite spectacular. The natural sight draws hundreds of visitors to Tickle Cove each summer. (Author photos)

2

So Help Me God!

No one had more than the other. Everyone had a job to live.

Theresa White

ALTHOUGH PROMISED BY the 1801 Act of Union agreement, Catholic freedom was not obtained in Ireland until 1829. This was another reason why so many Irish fled to the shores of Newfoundland. Here Catholics were permitted to openly practice their faith since the late 1700s.

Despite centuries of hatred, primarily based on religious intolerance, English Protestant (Church of England, later the Anglican Church of Canada), Irish Roman Catholic, and Methodist (later the United Church of Canada) immigrants found their way to the compromising shores of Tickle Cove. Others moved from overcrowded fishing centres such as Bonavista and the many islands of Bonavista Bay. With survival at the forefront, for the most part everyone got along.

Church of England surnames included Russell, Taylor, Cross, Skiffington, and Candow. The Overs were of United faith while the Legges, Kellys, Lanes, Maloneys, Mulcaheys, and Whites were of Roman Catholic descent.

The Roman Catholic priest served his worshippers twice a year at Tickle Cove and services were held at various shops and stores, even the local school. Other than that, Tickle Cove Catholics went to Mass at the Roman Catholic Church in Open Hall. Church of England worshippers attended church in Red Cliff.

A popular hymn recalled by Tickle Cove's eldest is "*O God, Our Help in Ages Past.*" Captain John Russell, one-hundred years old, learned it in his "early days" and sang it many times while sitting on his foster mother's knee. It was a common song heard from Christians in times of despair.

The peaceful existence between community and church is strongly visible at Tickle Cove, Red Cliff, and Open Hall today. The year 2004 marked the 100th anniversary of the Roman Catholic Church in Open Hall. Residents from all three communities worked alongside contractors hired to remodel the building to its original form. Captain Russell summed up the relationship.

"They always had that kind of attitude towards their church in my day as a young man. Church and the clergy always came first, regardless of anything else. It was as if it was planted in one's body. When a man started to pay

The Roman Catholic Church in Open Hall has served the people of Tickle Cove for over 100 years. (Author photo)

his church, he also started to regard the church as his personal property and therefore was always ready to help when needed."

Although courting, or "keeping company," as it is referred to in the Tickle Cove area, was not permitted between members of opposing religions, it still took place. The few inter-religious marriages were never soon forgotten. The christening of children refuelled old fires within one or both families. It was not unheard of for a family member to be disowned by a parent for marrying a person of a different faith, for it was often considered a "mortal sin" to commit such an act.

Despite the fact Catholics and Anglicans shared the same school, they still lived on opposite sides of the harbour. They attended each other's funerals but were forbidden to enter the church, or even the churchyard. In spite of this, the strength of ancient rules has diminished with time and never held the power to separate the neighbourhood. Captain Russell remembers more people fighting within their own religions than outside.

"My God! We danced together, ate together, and there was never a word. I can never remember a falling-out between a Protestant and a Catholic."

TIME FOR SCHOOL

Until the mid-1920s, in addition to their primary purpose, schools were utilized for religious services, funerals, and dances, better known as "times" in outport Newfoundland. Schooling was first introduced to the Tickle Cove area around 1830. At this time, schoolmaster and lay reader Thomas Walley taught at Tickle Cove itself under the sponsorship of the Society for the Propagation of the Gospel, an extension of the Church of England. The first school built at Tickle Cove, a one-room building, was located in a garden near the end of a gravel road in the town.

The first education Act in Newfoundland was introduced in 1836. Tickle Cove was awarded a school because it had the highest population in the area at the time. Former Bonavista-based policeman John Skiffington was appointed schoolmaster in May 1837. He taught school there until he retired for health reasons in 1868.

A lack of funding and a shortage of teachers and pupils made it virtually impossible for each settlement to maintain its own full-time school. Teachers alternated between Red Cliff, Open Hall, and Tickle Cove for periods of three months at a time. Children first attended school at Tickle Cove until a school was built at Red Cliff around 1863. This lasted until 1878 when classes were moved back to Tickle Cove.

Tickle Cove's school was closed in the spring of 1881 when teacher Catherine Flynn was transferred to a new school at Sweet Bay. It reopened in July 1882 with the appointment of a Miss Murphy, who stayed only until November of that same year. King's Cove native and teacher Ellen Sullivan, who had been stationed at Open Hall since early 1882, reopened the school at Tickle Cove nearly a year later.

Although Open Hall had been subjected to organized educational practices since the arrival of Henry Miles in 1863, the community first received an official school in 1883. It was not open long before it was forced to close due to a lack of money. Mary Matthews, the teacher of the short-lived school, filled the shoes of Ms. Sullivan at Tickle Cove from 1884 to 1887. The next teacher, or schoolmistress, as they were called, was Cecelia Flynn, followed by Catherine Hollohan, and Catherine Downey for the next four years until 1892. Maria Long and Ellen Moss held the position at various times until the end of the nineteenth century. Maggie Devine taught there in 1900, followed by Tickle Cove native Annie Mulcahey who taught there until 1903, spending the next two school years at a new one-room school constructed at Tickle Cove in 1904.

Anne Murphy, daughter of Keels merchant John Murphy, taught there from around 1910 to 1912 when she died of a cold. She was replaced by Mary Lawton of King's Cove, who taught there until 1915. Teacher Elizabeth Snow taught school at Tickle Cove until 1921.

Visiting teachers were housed by local families. Gertrude Maloney kept teachers for many years from King's Cove, Plate Cove, Sweet Bay, and as far away as Bay de Verde, Conception Bay North.

By 1921, there were only a dozen or so students at

Tickle Cove. Because of this, government was unwilling to fund schooling for the usual duration of ten months. Once again, they opted for a three-month spell of learning.

With the help of several local men, Tickle Cove's second school was built in 1904 under the supervision of King's Cove carpenter John Martin. It closed *circa* 1953. (Courtesy of Gertrude Maloney)

After grade six, students had the choice to "sit for examination." The four years of study to follow were known as Preliminary, Intermediate, Associate A, and Associate B, equivalent to grades nine, ten, eleven, and twelve today. In most cases, children became important contributors to the workload of their families and never returned to school after sixth grade.

After finishing Intermediate education at Open Hall in 1921, fifteen-year-old John Russell was asked to teach school at Tickle Cove. This request was normally carried out by the Anglican minister. With five students from Tickle Cove, and several more from Red Cliff, Russell taught school from the middle of June until mid-September at twenty-five dollars a month.

Former students of Russell's included Red Cliff's Jim Oldford, sisters Carrie and Millie Bowen, Tickle Cove's Joe Cross, brothers Roland and Jim Russell, and Gladys, Nellie, and John Over. The remainder of his pupils moved away to the United States with their parents and siblings following the tidal surge which struck the town just six weeks after school ended that year.

Lessons taught at school during this time included arithmetic, grammar, hygiene, history, and geography. An hour of reading from the Bible, called Scripture History, was also part of the course outline.

Some of Russell's favourite moments as a teacher at Tickle Cove were spent playing games with his pupils, half of whom were friends near his own age. During morning recess, he showed the younger children how to play games such as Tidley, Marbles, and Buttons.

Other teachers who alternated between local schools in the early days included Jessie Quinton, Blanche Taylor, Anne Cross, Olive Bowen, Elizabeth Hobbs, and Gwendolyn Pittman.

One-room schools were heated by a pot-belly stove. Students took turns carrying an armload, or "yaffle," of shavings, splits, or junks of wood to school every morning. Mostly boys would light the fire. For a little fun and excitement, it was quite common for one or two lads

Darrell Duke

Tickle Cove's last schoolhouse is used as a community centre today. (Author photo)

to get up on the roof of the school before the teacher arrived in the morning and to stuff the chimney with boughs, or to cover it with a brin bag. When it reached the top of the chimney, smoke was forced back down and out through the stove, filling the classroom and giving students time off until it was fit to go back inside. Almost every student hoped for such an event on a daily basis.

The third and last school built at Tickle Cove opened around 1954. It was near the pond on the property once owned by Annie and Paddy Kelly. Also a one-room building, it closed its doors to schooling in 1969 when students were transferred to King's Cove.

3

Communications and Transportation

We'd be walkin' over fences and it'd be the same as walkin' on the floor.

Theresa White, on the amount of snow in winter.

THE FIRST POST office at Tickle Cove opened in 1891 under the supervision of postmaster, and constable, Adam Skiffington, the son of former schoolmaster John Skiffington. Following the death of the younger Skiffington in 1911, the post office was taken over by his daughter-in-law, Sarah Walsh, the first of a long list of women who held the position.

In the early 1900s, Tickle Cove received its first telegraph. The heart of communications, as it was at the time, was located in the town's post office. If someone wanted to send a message outside the town, they told it to or wrote it down for the post office operator in Tickle Cove, who called the message to the operator at the post and telegraph office in King's Cove. From there, Morse code carried the message to its destination. The front page of the *Daily News* featured a segment called "By Telegraph," from which the following message appeared April 24, 1928:

> Harold Russell of Tickle Cove, while gunning on Friday morning had the thumb of his left hand blown off.

World and local news, followed by the next day's forecast, was also transmitted by Morse code to telegraph offices. If someone could not read, it was read to them by the post office operator.

Although currency was switched from the British mode to the decimal system in 1865, Newfoundland businesses and consumers continued to conduct transactions using the former system into the 1890s. The following is a list of postal prices taken from a record book used by a Fox Harbour merchant in 1884:

> *Inland Letters.* Not exceeding 4 oz. = 1d., 6 oz. = 1.5 d. (and so on at the rate of a halfpenny for every two ounces).
>
> *Parcel Post.* Not exceeding 1 lb. = 3d., 2 lb. = 4d. (ten lbs. cost one shilling).
>
> *Telegrams.* Twelve words = 6d. Each word above twelve cost an additional halfpenny. Delivery within three miles was free.

Money Orders. Not exceeding £1 cost 2d.; between £1 and £2 cost 3d., etc.

Newfoundland first issued stamps in 1857. After switching to decimal currency, new stamps were issued to the island in November 1868 in the form of a two-cent stamp depicting the codfish. A five-cent stamp showing a seal was used to pay the colonial rate for mail within the island. A ten-cent stamp, depicting Prince Alfred, was issued to pay the rate to the United States. A twelve-cent stamp, depicting Queen Victoria, was issued to pay the most common rate to Great Britain. A thirteen-cent stamp, depicting a fishing schooner, was issued to pay the rate to Canada, Cape Breton, New Brunswick, and St. Pierre et Miquelon. A one-cent stamp, depicting the Prince of Wales (later King Edward VII), was issued to pay the St. John's local delivery rate. In July 1870, stamps of three cents and six cents, featuring Queen Victoria, reflecting reduced rates for inland mail, as well as mail for Britain appeared. The last pre-Confederation stamp was issued on June 23, 1947.

Succeeding Sara Walsh as postmistress was Anne Cross, who housed the office in John Lane's home. After John Maloney, Gertrude Maloney carried on the service in her own home from 1953 to the end of 1969. From that time until 2003, the post office was operated by Ellen Lane, followed by Margarite Clements.

Confederation with Canada in 1949 brought about a major increase in mail. Mrs. Maloney remembers the boost, especially Simpson Sears and Eaton's orders.

The post office provided entertainment in the form of the *Family Fireside* (1924–1958), a free monthly magazine published by Gerald S. Doyle containing provincial news, household trivia, serial fiction, poetry, and social news.

Once mail arrived by train at Princeton, Alfred Prince would carry the mail in his horse-drawn wagon as far as Plate Cove. At this destination, "Uncle" Paddy Kelly took outgoing mail for Tickle Cove, Red Cliff, and Open Hall. He had a Newfoundland pony named "Minnie" which people joked suited him because it was very old and slow. Uncle Paddy off-loaded the outgoing mail to Prince, and picked up his area's portion of the load in return.

Prince's son, Jack, later took over his father's responsibilities. Years latter, he delivered mail by truck. Following the younger Prince, Jim Kelly of Tickle Cove and Red Cliff's Jack Hobbs delivered the mail for the area.

Letters for sailors and fishermen at sea were delivered by Newfoundland Railway coastal boats such as the *Glencoe*, or the *Argyle*, whose primary responsibility was to deliver supplies to outport communities. Letters picked up by coastal boats during their routine runs were posted to the name of the schooner with no fixed address. Usually the phrase "Somewhere on the Labrador" was stated as the schooner's whereabouts. Receiving a letter at sea eased the distance between fishermen and loved ones at home. At least in the heart.

The Tickle Cove post office, along with hundreds of others in Canada, is currently under the threat of closure as it is deemed an unfeasible operation due to the town's small population. As the fight for rural Newfoundland continues, residents are once again petitioning government in an effort to keep an essential service in their community.

THE PRINCETON TRAIN STATION

The train station at Princeton served as a key link between Tickle Cove and the rest of the province. Whether visiting relatives or seeking employment in St. John's, you were always sure to meet someone, or something, to occupy your arrival or departure time at the station.

Annie Kelly, ninety-four, remembers a frosty morning in the 1940s following a visit to her sister's home in St. John's. The only passenger to step off the train at 4:00 a.m., she made her way into the station's waiting room while the station manager, Adams, remained in his office. A little while later, a white billy goat strolled into the waiting room to "take a spell" and to escape winter's cold. Every goat for himself. Nobody objected.

The routine went something like this. At 6:00 a.m., Adams carried Kelly via horse and buggy to meet Sam Prince. Switching horses and buggies, Kelly was taken to Plate Cove West to again switch buggies for the last trip back to Tickle Cove with her husband, Sam. It was of no use to be in a hurry.

The Princeton train station also played a pivotal role in ensuring fish catches reached destinations abroad and

The train station at Princeton, Bonavista Bay, was a major link between people and businesses of Tickle Cove and the outside world for generations. (Courtesy of Fisheries' Library, Department of Fisheries and Oceans)

necessary fishing supplies arrived on time. When supplies came for the Quinton business in Red Cliff, Alfred Prince transported the goods by horse and cart to the wharf at Princeton.

It took ninety minutes by motorboat to get from Red Cliff to Princeton. Sometimes it took longer, depending on weather conditions. On one occasion, Quinton's boat got tangled in a salmon net during a nasty storm. After a while, the stern was turned into the wind and it got clear of the near-fatal trap. No matter how hard the wind blew, the trip had to be made.

The first Tickle Cove resident to own an automobile was Michael Austin Connors, *circa* 1925. The sole owner of modern transportation graciously drove people abroad when they had doctor's appointments and other important errands.

When the Reid Newfoundland Company first became involved with steamship services, it employed the firm of A. & J. Inglis in Glasgow, Scotland, to build the SS *Bruce*, the largest of a fleet of steamers known as the Alphabet Fleet. The *Bruce*, following the railway agreement of 1898, began Newfoundland's first passenger service to the Canadian mainland from Jerseyside, Placentia Bay, to Halifax, Nova Scotia. Later, it served the Tickle Cove area out of Open Hall, among other coastal steamers.

The area received electricity in 1965. A general telephone exchange was granted in 1969. The road connecting Open Hall, Red Cliff, and Tickle Cove first

Tickle Cove's first car, purchased by Michael Austin Connors. Aside from a few alders in the interior, the vehicle remains intact in a garden at Open Hall. (Author photo)

received asphalt in 1977, much earlier than other regions of rural Newfoundland.

The Newfoundland Railway coastal steamers *Bruce*, *Dundee*, *Malakoff*, and *Glencoe* docked at Open Hall since 1900, providing transportation to St. John's and all stops in between. The SS *Bruce*, pictured here, sank in 1911. (Courtesy of Newfoundland and Labrador Provincial Archives)

Provincially, to a great degree, the desire for social interaction has been strangled by the dirty hands of modernization. People tend to be colder and more withdrawn. The handwritten-with-care letter is dying a quick death to email. Bills are paid from the home through computers. Newfoundland's horizons are no longer dotted with schooners and steamers. The backs of old men are no longer visible along shorelines as there is not much to anticipate or discuss. Lonesomeness prevails.

A large house, once a home to a large family, and a yard once busy await summer visitors in Tickle Cove. (Author photo)

The welcomed rumble of the train has been replaced by the racket of ATVs en route to disrupt what is left of our bakeapple and blueberry marshes. Badly paved roads show no signs of smiling men in horse-powered carts. Disgruntled, quasi-criminal taxi drivers have replaced friendly neighbours with vehicles.

At Tickle Cove there is a conscious effort to draw visitors to old ways and old days. In this case, there is opportunity for a future in the past.

4

Living With the Sea

Stages and flakes: you never thought you'd see the day they'd be no more.

Captain John Russell

THE AMOUNT OF work necessary to survive daily in the early years of Newfoundland settlement is barely comprehensible, especially when compared to the comforts of life today. While modernization has lessened the burden of a family, it has also created a laziness dominating a large portion of the present population. Without the distraction of the television, telephone, and computer, all hands played a pivotal role in the task of survival. Free from the unfair class systems of their European forefathers, all residents and neighbours of Tickle Cove were considered equal and worked together in a manner almost non-existent in today's modern world. When earning a dollar surpassed its purpose of providing life's requirements, priorities became muddled. As a result, communities divided, all competing for a share of the so-called "better life" dominating larger centres.

The people of Tickle Cove stuck to the basics of life, creating a clear window to a rapidly fading cultural heritage. This allowed both present and future genera-tions a chance to appreciate the positive attitude and strong work ethic of those who walked before them.

Not all men were great boat builders in the early days of Newfoundland settlement. However, there were a lot who had no trouble finding the right trees to cleverly carve ribs for a ship's hull. Tickle Cove was never short of case-hardened handymen and heavy-duty sailors. If most of the time was spent at sea, a good boat was needed. Various styles of boats emerged to prosecute an ever-changing fishery. Adaptation to migratory patterns of fish was of utmost importance. Boats were such a personal part of a family's life, in discussion they are still referred to as "she."

Every family built their own boat to suit themselves. The most common boat used for the inshore fishery was the "punt," also known as a "rodney" in some parts of Bonavista Bay. Capable of handling all sorts of weather, Captain Russell described the punt's length to vary from "fourteen to eighteen feet." It was fairly easy to row and made great sailing before or across the wind. In addition to two eight-foot oars, a twelve-foot "scull" oar was used with one hand to prevent drifting while the other hand was free to jig cod, or "fish." A sail was added when the wind was suitable. Boys often learned to row a punt before their teens. In all sorts of weather, punts were used to tend traps, gill nets, and trawls. They were a means of transportation for church-goers and a great ticket for providing romantic getaways for couples keeping company. In winter, when pack ice and slush, or "slob" covered the sea, punts were "the real thing" for hunting birds and seals. Two young men could easily pull a punt over ice pans or row through slob ice. The punt was later changed to a four-oared, two-sailed boat.

The handline, or "hook and line" the fishermen used, was a double-hooked, fish-shaped piece of lead called a jigger, with bait. They required three men to a boat. The men rose at 3:00 a.m., had a meal and left the stagehead around four o'clock for the five to six-mile trip to the outside fishing grounds. Lunch sacks were packed the night before. If the caplin were in, a quick trip to the beach with a "cast" net guaranteed fresh bait. When it came time to use the trawls, they went to the squid-jigging grounds for fresh bait.

Cod seines were long nets shot around schools of cod in shoal water. Propelled by oar and sail, seine or "trap" skiffs, twenty-five to thirty-five feet in length, were required to handle such bulky nets. Four men tended to the nets in punts towed behind a trap skiff. They then returned to the skiff to unload their catch. By 1845, nine seines were in use at Tickle Cove. In 1857, 4,526 quintals of fish were reportedly caught by fishermen in the community.

When cod moved offshore, up to a distance of fifteen miles, large, seaworthy boats were required. Rigged with permanent masts, the seine skiff was changed to a "bully." The Bonavista Bay bully was a small, decked schooner, ranging twenty-five to thirty-five feet in length and weighing twelve to sixteen tons. If the wind was abeam, the bully's mainsail, foresail, and jib were used. Oars were used on a calm day.

While fishing inshore, men used what they referred to as "marks" (positions between geographic landmarks) to indicate the area they wanted to fish. Fishermen agreed upon and used marks visible from their boats to avoid confrontation over who fished where. The following marks were those of the late Samuel Kelly of Tickle Cove.

Other marks worthy of mention include the following:

Rock in Raymond's Garden
Sheep in Tickle
2nd Window Roland's House
Rock Below Stable

If the fog was in and a fisherman could not see one of his marks, he wrote something similar to the following:

Foggy, Ben's Green not out

TO THE LABRADOR

By the 1840s, an increase in fishermen and a decrease in cod stocks inevitably sent men farther abroad to fish. As distance from home increased, a larger vessel was required. For this reason, the age of the Labrador "schooner" began. Ranging from thirty to 100 tons, schooners were built for carrying capacity, rather than for speed.

When handling a schooner, sailors "cut down her sails" according to how much abuse she could handle from wind and wave. A schooner then adhered to the sea. If too much canvas was kept on her in heavy wind, damage and often disaster could be expected.

A schooner's skipper took his men "in collar," or

hired them, around the twentieth of May. They left around the third week in June (also known as "collar day") and, if they were lucky, they returned the last of August with a full load of fish.

Wind and weather determined how long it took a schooner to reach its destination on the Labrador. With a good southwest wind, they were guaranteed to make it across the 'Straits' of Belle Isle in three days. The Straits, a relatively narrow passage between the northern tip of Newfoundland and Labrador, is a treacherous place to navigate in threatening winds and has provided many a resting place for ships and sailors alike. "A good morning, with a good sou'west wind," will get you from Cape Norman, Newfoundland's most northwesterly point, to Cape Charles, Labrador, in four hours.

Fishermen tended to their traps in dories normally containing a mariner's compass, two quarts of drinking water per man, solid food, and a foghorn or trumpet. The latter was often an unheard-of luxury, and was replaced by shouting when dories went astray in fog. The skipper was responsible for providing paint, traps, food or ("grub") for the trip, as well as salt for preserving the catch. The costs of these items were recouped by the skipper at the end of the trip. For example, if a voyage yielded 800 quintals of fish, at five dollars a quintal (roughly $4,000), when it was "made" and shipped, the skipper took half. The remaining $2,000 was divided evenly among the skipper and fishermen.

It was not unheard of for a crew to catch 800–900

quintals of cod in four weeks. If catches were scarce, a crew often had to go into ten or fifteen ports in search of enough fish to consider the trip worthwhile. The placing and hauling of traps meant a lot of hard work. Sometimes, a coastal boat reported lots of fish in a particular spot. Often, by the time a schooner reached the location, the fish were nowhere to be found. And so be it. It came with the life.

Tickle Cove had its fair share of schooners taking part in the Labrador fishery. According to vessel registration records, when a schooner was out of commission for good, whatever the reason, it was referred to as "closed out."

In 1844, farmer and planter Thomas Mullowney, and his sons, Thomas, Jr., William, John, and Edward built the *Thomas and Betsy*. The two-masted vessel was lost at sea in 1872. The following year they constructed the *Star*. This seventeen-ton schooner was lost at sea in 1884.

In 1856, John, James, Robert, and Richard Taylor built the *William and Mary*. The vessel reportedly "broke up" in 1877. In 1863, John and Richard Taylor constructed the *Margaret Jane*. Although the reason for her closing is not known, the schooner's official closure year is 1924. Though losses were high per capita, some schooners survived more than fifty years. Also in 1863, George Prince built a schooner named *Mary Ann*. Bonavista merchant James Ryan had the bully *Pearl* built at Tickle Cove in 1874. She was lost near Bonavista in 1880.

Tickle Cove's John Lane took part in the Labrador

The ruthlessness of Mother Nature is evident in this photo taken at Twillingate, Notre Dame Bay, following the gale of September 17, 1907. In this scene, at least five schooners were thrown on the rocks while most wharves and stages were destroyed and carried away by the sea. In Tickle Cove, roughly thirty-five nautical miles away four schooners were wrecked. (Courtesy of Fisheries' Library, Department of Fisheries and Oceans)

fishery every year from 1890 to 1920. His first boat was the *Jubilee*. The farmer and planter had a schooner built at Tickle Cove in 1898. The *Five Brothers*, as she was called, was lost off the coast of Labrador on August 29, 1905. Lane's third vessel, *Bert*, was built in Bay Bulls in 1902. Skippered by his brother, Thomas, it was wrecked while moored at Tickle Cove in the September 17 gale of 1907, a storm which brought a lot of schooners to their resting places along the province's northeast coast. It was this same storm which claimed two acres of land from Kelly's Island, Conception Bay South.

The *Mary Ann*, owned by Thomas White, was also destroyed in the September 1907 gale, along with a boat belonging to Cornelius Kelly. It is not known whether White's schooner was the same *Mary Ann* built by George Prince in 1863 because Prince's boat did not close until 1924 for reasons unknown. It is quite possible, however, the boat was salvaged and repaired. The collector schooner the *Evelyn*, built and owned by Bonavista merchant Philip Templeman in Sweet Bay in 1905, was lost at sea in the same storm while moored off Tickle Cove. The schooner contained 250 quintals of dried fish.

John Lane also skippered the *Cabot Content*, a twenty-ton vessel built at Random Sound, Trinity Bay, in 1897. The vessel, owned by George Burfeit of Random Sound, ran ashore fully loaded with supplies at Tickle Cove in 1912. Covered by insurance, she was a total loss. Lane's last assignment was on the *Flora*, a schooner built by St. John's Merchant Charles Steer at Noggin Cove, Notre Dame Bay, in 1904. The boat was used until 1951. Another of John Lane's brothers, Charles, was captain of the *Spring Bird*.

Other schooners belonging to Tickle Cove men included the *Foam*, owned by Thomas White, and the *Pelican*, owned by Benjamin Russell, who was also in charge of the *Columbia*. William Russell fished the Labrador as captain of the *Turtle*. Another well-known vessel operator of Tickle Cove was John Kelly. Prior to 1908, Kelly operated the *Fair Wind*, a boat owned by Plate Cove West's Richard Fennell. She was constructed at King's Cove in 1899. In 1908, Kelly, along with his sons, Joe, Ronald, and Ignatius, took charge of the *Mary C*. This boat also belonged to Fennell and was built by Edward Mullowney at Sweet Bay for the Ryan business of Bonavista. She closed in 1943 for reasons unknown.

The most familiar schooner name to residents of the Tickle Cove area is that of the *Tishy*, belonging to the merchant Quintons of Red Cliff.

Tickle Cove's long-time friend and neighbour, Jim Oldford of Red Cliff, is highly commended for his contributions to boat building in the area. Now a sturdy man of ninety-three, he built twenty-one boats in as many winters.

CLOSE CALL AT SEA

In 1945, Captain John Russell bought the schooner *Flora MacIvor* from the Warehams of Harbour Buffett, Placentia Bay. While getting his schooner ready for coasting, Russell was assigned the task of bringing a load of sand from Sandy Harbour, Harbour Buffett, to St. John's.

With a beautiful northerly wind, captain and crew sailed out of Harbour Buffett in the morning. Rounding Cape St. Mary's, coming out of Placentia Bay with hopes of reaching Trepassey in St. Mary's Bay, the wind chopped from the southeast. A "livin' gale" ripped every sail from the wooden boat, with the exception of the foresail and jumbo. They ran in under the cliffs below Cape St. Mary's light in search of shelter and let the anchor go. In less than an hour, the anchor chain broke off right to the bow. It was six o'clock in the evening and they were adrift in the middle of an angry sea. Hard-pressed by the northeast winds of Placentia Bay, they drifted all night. "There was nothing we could do but put on the kettle," Russell said.

The next evening, the wind dropped out and veered from the northwest. Through dead reckoning, Captain Russell speculated a course for Cape Race lighthouse. Between midnight and 1:00 a.m. all hands were relieved by the sight of the land light. The *Flora MacIvor* had drifted southeast of the French islands of St. Pierre et Miquelon, roughly fifty miles off their original course. According to Captain Russell, "'Twas only by God and by guess" they survived the ordeal. "'Twas a very good shot," he said.

In May, fishermen started working the herring scull. Herring nets were set in the water each evening and "looked at" the next morning. In 1857, forty-seven barrels of herring were taken at Tickle Cove.

Around the middle of June, caplin began rolling in on beaches to spawn. Cod, feeding on caplin, followed the smaller fish to the beaches. This provided a great boost to the inshore fishery.

The salmon fishery required nets about fifty fathoms (300 feet) deep. Set from the shoreline, they were checked once at morning, noon, and evening. This ceased around the end of June when fishermen finally saw money for their hard work. When the day of reckoning came for the selling of salmon, fishermen made anywhere from eighty to 120 dollars, amounts which carried families up to October when returns from the cod fishery helped settle up credit advances by the merchants.

Lobster harvesting became a sure source of income in Tickle Cove in the late 1800s. With line-knit doors for them to enter, lobsters were coaxed inside wooden cages by a dangling herring or cod.

The first lobster canning factory was put into practice in Atlantic Canada around 1870. Records indicate a canning business, operated by Joseph Lane, was located near the brook flowing into Tickle Cove harbour around 1910. The following year twenty-four cases of lobster were recorded at Tickle Cove.

The seine skiff evolved into the motorboat. The weight of a motor required a boat to have a stronger stern and a flatter bottom. Because motorized boats could travel farther distances, meaning longer periods away from land, a shelter or "cuddy" was added to the front of boats. This space usually contained a small stove or "bogey" for both warmth and cooking.

In the early 1900s, topsails and topmasts were replaced by small marine engines. Some engines used an igniter, connected to a set of six batteries, while others used a sparkplug. Igniter engines, also known as "Make 'n' Break" engines, included the Atlantic, Acadia, and Mianus. Sparkplug engines included the Gray, Lathrop, and Coaker, named after the founder and long-time president of Newfoundland's Fishermen's Protective Union, William Coaker.

On a grander scale, steam trawlers were introduced on the Grand Banks in 1911. Although Newfoundland proposed a treaty to ban trawling, it was rejected by England, stating the move seemed ". . . premature and unjustifiable."

Circa 1913, John Lane was the first to own a boat engine in Tickle Cove. It was a Mianus. Around 1918, brothers Arch and John Skiffington owned the first Coaker in Tickle Cove. At this time, a small marine engine cost about two to three hundred dollars. A man could locate a "knock" in a boat engine by touching a lead pencil, held between his teeth, on various parts of the motor.

The Newfoundland cod trap was developed in the 1870s. Roughly sixty fathoms on the round, a cod trap is square containing a long wall-like "leader" which, from the mouth of the trap, extends toward shore. The codfish is, as some would say, "as foolish as a bag of nails." This almost always guarantees the fish will follow the leader into the trap and stay there. The cod trap ensured a few hours' sleep nightly for men, and was mentally refreshing to them because it was an easy way to secure a voyage when fish were plentiful. It was also considered safer due to the fact you were never a long way from home.

Beginning in early July, men did not rise until 5:00 a.m. They would have a lunch and leave to haul the trap around six o'clock. Once a boatload of fish was caught, they motored back and a couple of fellows threw the fish up on the stagehead with a fish fork, or "pew." The other two men went home and had breakfast. They put away the fish when they returned to the stagehead. The other two were then relieved to eat breakfast.

Because the longest distance from shore was only a mile or so, wives, mothers, and sisters prepared a solid breakfast for their breadwinner's return. A common breakfast was a fresh fish put away from the day before. There was no such thing as going to the store and buying a pound of ham and a dozen eggs. Families kept hens and, usually, the local merchant had a side of bacon or a couple of hams about twice a month. Because there was no refrigeration, food of this nature was often spoken for before it arrived. There was little fear of not getting a fresh meal.

Unmarried men depended on their mothers for a breakfast of boiled bread with fish, commonly referred to in Newfoundland as "fish 'n' brewis." Other times she had beans, cooked the previous night, or fried cod tongues.

The middle of the day was not a good time to "haul" fish. The mornings or evenings were best, depending, of course, on the tide. It was pointless going out at low tide, because the water went out and the fish went with it. When the tide returned in the evening, the fish eventually came with it. That is when a lot of fish ended up in the cod trap.

Around 4:00 p.m. men ate an early supper and were headed to the trap by five o'clock. After three hours or so, the fish was aboard the boat. Then it was back to the lamplit stage for unloading, heading, splitting, and salting. If eighteen to twenty quintals of fish were hauled, men stayed up into the middle of the night, often only a few hours before they had to return to the trap. It was not uncommon for men to stay up all night at the fish with no rest. If there was an hour to spare, from the time the fish were put away until it was time to go to the trap again, men went home and napped on the kitchen settle. Some lay on the floor near the stove. Staying near the stage was not a common practice as the change was considered as good as the rest.

At the stagehead, one fellow put the fish on the cutting table. Another cut the fish's throat and passed it along to the next man who, with two moves, removed the head. After the fourth man split the fish, removing its insides, all four joined in to salt the fish, ensuring it did not spoil. Salt, like most necessities, was obtained from the local merchant. The entire preparation process was referred to as "making" fish. When the fish was made, and cleaning up or "clearing away" was done, it was back to the cod trap by noon.

Only the wind prevented men from attending their nets. If the wind was "in on the shore," with a twenty-mile-per-hour breeze, they did not bother. If wind was less than that, they checked their traps. Fear of wind derived almost solely from the possibility of disrupting the boat and trap. Fear for their lives was never the primary concern.

If there were twenty quintals of fish, it was salted enough so it could stand a few days of bad weather once spread on the flakes to dry. A "flake" consisted of big beams shored up horizontally, eight or ten feet apart and topped with closely placed "longers" (long trees, narrow in diameter and skinned of their branches and bark). Some people spread spruce boughs on top, while others spread the fish out on the bare longers. Flakes were built above stores and stages to avoid shading, and close to the water so fish benefited from cool ocean breezes, in turn, reducing the threat of sunburn. Where possible, fish were also spread on large beach rocks to dry. This practice, of course, was favoured by local cats.

In the evenings, after a couple of weeks of salting, fish was washed out in a vat called a water horse. It was then packed in the stage, where the water ran down through the longers. The next morning, if the weather was suitable, fish was carried up on the flakes. The term "water horse" also refers to a stack of split and salted cod when it is piled in layers to drain after washing.

If the fish got one good day on the flakes, it was considered fair. After two good days, one could say it was made. When ready, fish was carried to the local store for sale according to its grade. The grading or "culling" of fish, like all aspects of business, followed strict guidelines.

Sunburned fish was known as "West Indies," or "cullage." This occurred when fish was taken out of the water horse, carried up on the flakes in the morning and spread before it had a chance to dry. Basically, the fish boiled in the sun, turning it to crud while still wet inside.

Then there was "maggoty" fish. People may recognize the term from the traditional Newfoundland song, *I'se the B'y*. "I don't want your maggoty fish / That's no good for winter / I can get me better than that / Down in Bonavista." This grade develops after flies stow away in a bulk of fish. For days the flies eat the fish, leaving their spit behind, which eventually becomes a maggot. Often, before the problem is recognized, millions of maggots have accumulated. By this time the nape, where the head was removed, is eaten away. The merchant still gave the "number two" price for maggoty fish because the rest of the fish was fit to eat.

Merchants from St. John's sent men known as "collectors" in schooners to the Tickle Cove area to buy fish for the Spanish market. Lightly salted cod with a yellow cast caught in October or "late trawl fish," was popular in the Spanish markets. Prices reached twenty-seven dollars a quintal. This price, compared to five and six dollars per quintal for trap fish, was considered incredible. Men spent the better part of fall packing fish for this market.

Although there has been a somewhat lucrative crab fishery in recent years, the wiry crustacean was once considered a nuisance, always tangling in gear used to catch cod. Crab was never considered edible by the older folks at Tickle Cove, but, on occasion, young boys roasted the odd one by the waterside.

Fishing accidents were sparse at Tickle Cove. Everyone was careful not to load down their boats with too much fish. Men kept an eye on what is referred to as "freeboard" when taking fish. When a boat is sitting in the water on a calm day, there is roughly six to ten inches from the top of the boat to the water's surface. If it was blowing, common sense was applied.

After July, cod traps were hauled up and placed on the beach, or "bawn," to dry. When dried, nets were brushed to get rid of seaweed and kelp. Then they were stored away for the winter.

Men spent a week or two in August doing things for themselves. If a small store, cellar, or fence had to be built, this was the time to do it.

During the last week of August, squid began to appear. When they showed signs of "gettin' big," it was time to go trawling for bait. A squid is an odd creature. One can never be certain of its next move. It moves backwards or "arse-formus" (foremost), as it is known in Newfoundland. It has fins on its tail end, like propellers. A squid is attracted to the colour red, hence the colour of a squid-jigger. An old-fashioned squid jigger consisted of hooks stuck in a piece of lead about three inches long, roughly the diameter of your middle finger. When a squid sees a jigger, it wraps its tentacles around it. Bait is unnecessary. When not being pursued, squid are known to lounge around. In the days when squid were plentiful, there were lots everywhere. If they were scarce in one spot, they were scarce everywhere. They were in great demand by the Chinese markets. Many folks fondly recall being down at the flakes at night in lantern light putting squid on poles to dry.

When squid were scarce, fishermen resorted to digging clams, or "cocks and hens" as they are often called in parts of Newfoundland. When the tide went out and a hole appeared in the muddy floor, it meant there was a clam there.

There were usually fifty hooks to a line and six lines to a tug. If you were lucky enough to have the tide on your side and to dig 300 clams, it was time to move on. Spring tides, or "springes" occur twice in each lunar month. Because tides rise the highest and fall to the lowest level from the mean tide point, boats were more easily launched or hauled up at this time.

Proper clothing to ensure the most comfort possible while fishing was a necessity. Oil clothes were made out of flour sacks and saturated in linseed oil for waterproofing. Even the Cape Ann, a fisherman's oilskin cap named after Cape Ann, Massachusetts, was made by women in this fashion. All clothes, including knitted

All in a life's work. Joseph Legge of Tickle Cove with a load of freshly caught cod. (Courtesy of Mike and Marge O'Shea)

socks, shirts, vamps, and drawers, were made by women of the community.

By October it was usually pretty cold. Men got out of their warm beds around 2:00 a.m., put on their oil clothes (later replaced by rubber clothes and boots), and headed down to the stagehead and got aboard their boats. They motored a mile, sometimes a mile and a half, to the squid-jigging grounds as cold, salty water steadily blew on their hands and faces. The man handling the engine did not wear mitts. Only the man at the tiller steering the boat wore his double-knitted handmade mitts. Catching squid for bait, which usually came to a halt around the twentieth of October, often stretched well into the month of November.

A family's provisions for the winter usually included 100 pounds of made fish, half-barrels of herring, turbot, and cod's heads, plus a dozen salted salmon. Stuffed fresh squid also provided a scrumptious meal.

Although women of Tickle Cove did not go on the water, they played a vital role in the fishery. Aside from homemaking duties and farming, women worked long hours once fish were landed. If men were still catching fish when the drying process began, making the fish was the sole responsibility of the women.

Depending on the method in which her husband or son was catching fish, a woman's role varied. In the days of handlining, there may have only been one boatload of fish a day to put away. With the small crew executing several tasks apiece, a woman did not always have to participate. In addition to assisting in the making of fish, a trapman's wife prepared and served several meals daily. A skipper's wife was in charge when her husband was away. She was responsible for deciding whether or not fish was put out, and how much was spread out in the morning. She was aware of which fish piles were at varying degrees of curing. Also, like her husband, she knew all signs of "weather ahead." Women, to any great degree, did not get directly involved with the fishery until, primarily, the start of the crab craze in the early 1990s.

The First World War (1914–1918) had major implications for the world's fish market. As in all wars, the economy was the prime target, and Newfoundland fish was a major source of fuel for the market. Ships en route from Newfoundland to Central America were often victims of German submarines scurrying along the ocean floor of North America's Eastern Seaboard. By the middle of the war, foreign buyers of salt cod were paying up to twenty-six dollars a quintal; compared to the usual five or six dollars. A lot of fish was lost with ships torpedoed by German U-boats. Countless millions of dollars worth of cod were irretrievable.

The overfishing of cod, herring, squid, mackerel, and lobster by foreign countries painted a dismal picture for the remainder of the twentieth century. However, a peak season occurred in 1952 when cod landings off Newfoundland's coast reached 300,000 tons. Salmon catches produced unusually high numbers as well that year. Red Cliff merchants, the Quintons, prepared 224 cases of salmon for shipment in one day; a record untouched in the Tickle Cove area both before and after 1952.

Although the introduction of refrigeration helped deplete various fish and animal stocks, a fisherman's life was made easier because he had the option of bringing his catch to a cold storage facility and walking away with pay, as opposed to staying up all night making it and storing it away. Designed and pushed by the Japanese in the late 1930s as the answer to distribution problems of the fish trade, refrigeration marked the end of the traditional cod fishery. Smaller outfits could not keep up with the demand for fish and were eventually forced to close.

The Japanese also invented the gill net, a product greatly responsible for the demise of the fishery. When these small-meshed nets are discarded, they drift or get caught on the seabed. Known as "ghost nets," they continue to catch fish. When drifting gill nets become full, they sink and their contents rot. Then they drift again, and the killing continues.

The downfall of the Newfoundland fishery began in 1954 with the introduction of the first factory freezer trawler on the Grand Banks. With nets and rigging designed to haul up to sixty tons of fish at a time, the cod population, along with other species, never stood a chance. With a single blow, tons of cod and other species are dumped to factory decks, loaded on conveyor belts, and fed to filleting machines. Depending on the species of choice at the time, or a particular company's interests, unwanted, dead fish are returned to the sea, a certain end to processing plants in rural areas of the province as well.

The fishermen of Tickle Cove held on during the 1960s and 1970s. By 1968, foreign vessels were accounting for eighty-five per cent of the total catch. Inshore fishermen were catching only half the amount they caught in the 1950s. In 1970, the federal government advised cabinet to reduce the number of people involved with the Atlantic fishery. The proposal was rejected. Seven years later, Canada extended its jurisdiction to 200 miles, consequently leaving them with more waters to patrol.

As on land, the food chain of the sea requires little interruption to guarantee total chaos. In the 1980s, the federal government allowed an open season on the dragging of the caplin spawning grounds known as the Hamilton Banks. Initially carried out by Russian draggers, it was not long before the main food source of the marine ecosystem became almost non-existent. Caplin fed cod and sea birds alike. Once again, human greed had taken its toll on marine life.

Total allowable catches dropped drastically from 1983 to 1992 when then Federal Fisheries Minister John Crosbie announced a two-year ban on commercial fishing. In 1993, the ban was extended indefinitely. The following year, a compensation program called The Atlantic Groundfish Strategy, or TAGS was put into place with 45,000 qualifiers, most from Newfoundland. With the exception of a small, tourist-like "food fishery," open a few weeks in late summer, the cod fishery remains closed today.

Most Newfoundlanders are saddened that they cannot catch a fish for a meal without harsh consequences from government laws, the same government which set the standard for the demise in the first place.

Following more than a decade of fishing, the once-unfavoured crab, too, is making its way into the same sad fate which befell the codfish.

There was a day when Tickle Cove's eldest, most experienced fishermen never dreamed of a depletion of fish stocks. They cannot help but wonder what will happen next. Millions of pounds of cod, salmon, squid, and herring once brought to the shores of Bonavista Bay annually are now merely sour ingredients in rural conversation.

5

Sealing the Deal

When you fell through the ice, you'd be let back aboard long enough to change into dry clothes. Then it was back on the ice, the same as you'd heave a cat outdoors.

Captain John Russell

COLD, HARSH WINTERS brought opportunities for a fresh meal of seal. The most common seal hunted was the "harp." "Hood" and "square-flippered" seals were also hunted, but were not as plentiful. In the early years, "bedlamer" seals, too immature to breed, were shot, or caught in nets set from the shore, a practice which failed as young seals became scarce. Records indicate fifty-six seals were taken at Tickle Cove in 1845, while the next best year was 1874 when fifty-four were reportedly caught. While seal meat was shared among families, friends, and neighbours, pelts were put on ice and sold later in the spring, often in exchange for the substantial debt owing to the merchant. The demand for seal-fat oil was also high. Used since the late 1700s as a major source of lamp fuel, seal fat was also sold to lubricate machinery, and to cure leather. Following the American Revolution (1763–1775), when New England ceased to supply Britain with whale oil, the need for seal oil became paramount.

When harbours and inlets were clear of ice, men and boys shot seals from their boats. When ice was inland, they hunted seals among the pans and slob. These excursions sometimes ended in tragedy. In 1869, while sealing, James Taylor of Tickle Cove fell through the ice and drowned.

On the morning of March 7, 1924, following a winter storm, the entire coastline of Tickle Cove, Red Cliff, and Open Hall was blocked with ice. William Quinton, Sr. of Red Cliff decided to head out on the ice off Tickle Cove Point to look for seals. Around 8:00 a.m., Will, as he was known, headed out with knapsack and rifle in hand. That afternoon, seventeen-year-old John Russell and some friends made up their minds to take a chance and see if they could get a seal. People of all ages made their way out on the ice, but soon returned to land when the sea began to run in. Witnessing this, Russell and company decided to stay put on the shore. Everybody had landed except Will, who was not out of sight, but far away. People figured they would have to throw him a rope once he got in so far. They could see him just outside

Wester Rock, the breaking rock between Tickle Cove and Red Cliff. All of a sudden he disappeared. Some assumed he had spotted a seal and was lying low. Others thought the worst. The latter were right. Will had fallen through the ice, never to be seen again. People waited anxiously and in vain that night. It was a very traumatizing experience, especially when it was not safe to venture onto the moving ice to look for him. Around 7:00 p.m. the wind veered from the south. By eleven o'clock there was no sign of ice in the entire bay. That is when they knew for sure he had drowned.

When adult harp seals moved southward to bear their young, many Tickle Cove men gazed toward the Labrador coast in preparation for the dreaded sealing, or "swiling," as it was better known. First, men had to find a berth aboard a sealing ship. With provisions in tow, men took the train from Princeton to St. John's to join thousands of others in asking around the docks until a berth was secured. In the very early days of the seal fishery, men and ships headed out of Greenspond, Bonavista Bay.

The seal "fishery," as it is referred to today, was never considered reliable. One year could produce a "bumper crop," while another year a "jink." One spring, John Russell worked from March 10 to the last of April, on the SS *Ungava*. When he arrived back at port in St. John's, he had made twelve dollars. He paid $11.50 of it for his return train ticket home. "Top that for two months' hard work," he said.

Swiling was a deadly game dictated by sealing merchants and captains whose greed often surpassed regard for human life. The following excerpt is from Captain Russell, who spent six springs "to the ice," summarizing some of the events of a sealing trip to the Labrador.

"I believe we had one hundred and ten [men] on the *Sir John* [*Crosbie*]. Usually, when you'd strike the first seal, you'd probably get a nice, fair-sized patch, you know, probably four or five thousand [seals]. Then, the first thing you do is start killin' and peltin' 'em, and puttin' them on pans, a couple or 300 on a pan. When you got the patch cleaned up, you start pickin' up [pelts] then. If you [the crew] were jammed, the sealers had to get to work and haul them seals to her. Some would take, accordin' to the size of the man, two or three pelts. A smaller man would settle for two pelts. The most times, you didn't have to do much haulin'; the ship could penetrate the ice in lots of cases and get to the pans. All you had to do then was heave over your line then and pick 'em up . . . winch 'em in, you see.

"Sometimes you'd get jammed. Probably, there'd be about four or five hundred seals on that pan, but then you'd take the wire and go on. Four or five men would take the end of the wire and walk. They'd walk to the seals with the 'whip line' [a wire used to hoist seals aboard a ship]. They'd tie up, probably, twelve to sixteen [seals]. In the meantime, they had enough rope where they wouldn't have to come back for the whip line again. They'd tie on the end of the rope and let it go on."

The ship's first and second mates were normally always aboard the ship. In some cases, the second mate went out on the ice with the "common" sealers. The back line ran from the pelt-covered ice pan back to the ship. When a load of seals was dumped onto the ship's deck, a man stationed with the seals on the pan hauled the whip line back. This practice used the same mechanics as a clothesline. Before the walkie-talkie, communication between a master watch and the common sealer did not exist, unless they were in shouting distance of one another. If a master watch sighted snow clouds, or "skids," he warned the men on the ice to "heave 'er down" and to make their way back to the ship. When men were three and four miles from the ship, and the ship was jammed in ice, the danger of freezing rang loud and clear. Though it was cold, March provided better working conditions than April, when days were warmer and longer. The latter conditions brought with them the danger of a sealer's eyes becoming filled with sweat, often leaving him in tempo-rary blindness as cool winds and blowing snow froze his eyelids.

The Newfoundland steam sealing fleet consisted of nineteen ships. Two of these vessels, the *Neptune* and the *Nimrod*, were constructed under the supervision of Tickle Cove's Captain Edward White in Scotland.

White, born at Tickle Cove in 1811, moved to St. John's after 1830. Every spring from 1867 to 1871, White took the *Neptune* to the ice and continued as captain of the *Neptune* from 1873 to 1883. Sir William Vallance Whiteway was Newfoundland's prime minister for the terms of 1878–85, 1889–94, and 1895–97. White served as a minister in Whiteway's cabinet from 1882 to 1885, a period during which the Tickle Cove native introduced Newfoundland's first sealing legislation—offering sealers better incentives to take on the gruelling task each spring. White died in 1886.

ANDY MALONEY

Newfoundland had its share of sealing disasters, including the *Southern Cross* and the *Newfoundland*, both in 1914, the latter best described by the late Cassie Brown in her novel *Death on the Ice*. Andy Maloney of Tickle Cove was thirty-three years of age when he survived the *Greenland* disaster of 1898.

The steamship *Greenland* was built in Aberdeen, Scotland, in 1872 for the Montreal Steam and Fishing Company. The ship was later purchased by Newfoundland firm John Munn and Company for the purpose of partaking in the annual seal hunt. Always believed to have a curse, the *Greenland* had more than her share of bad luck. In 1884, while preparing for a trip to Labrador, the vessel caught fire and sank at her moorings in St. John's harbour. She was eventually refloated and put back to work.

The departure of sealers and ships for the great hunt

was a torturous time for families as thousands lined the St. John's waterfront bidding farewell to their brave men. On March 10, 1898, wishes of a "bumper trip" and "bloody decks" were cast by children and wives of sealers taking to the ice in several sealing vessels. Bonavista Bay accounted for 158 men, ranging from ages seventeen to forty-eight, out of 207 sealers aboard the *Greenland*, under the direction of Captain George Barbour. Accompanying the ill-fated ship were the steamers *Diana, Mastiff, Iceland, Aurora, Neptune,* and *Leopard.*

The next day, on March 21, caught out in a storm and separated from their ship, sealers from the *Greenland* were forced to take shelter, keeping warm from fires built from their gaffs and ropes. Some men, delusional from the experience and nature's elements, approached fellow sealers and invited them into their homes for a mug-up. The next minute the sealers vanished, never to be seen again. Weak-minded and snowblinded, many of the men wandered aimlessly, eventually falling through the ice to a frosty grave. One man kept from freezing by smearing seal blood over his exposed body parts.

During a break in the storm, about 100 men were rescued. Back on the ice, songs and hymns were sung to pass the time and to boost spirits. Men took turns lying on a live seal for its body heat. The seal was killed, roasted, and eaten the next morning. The storm abated thirty-six hours later as survivors made their way to the now visible and accessible ship. In the end, forty-eight men were dead. Of these, twenty-five bodies were recovered and twenty-three were never found.

This image of man-covered ice floes clearly indicates the risks of the annual seal hunt. The ill-fated *Florizel*, pictured here, was lost near Cappahayden on Newfoundland's Southern Shore on February 23, 1918. Ninety-four of the 144 persons on board perished. (Courtesy of Fisheries' Library, Department of Fisheries and Oceans)

On the way back, the *Greenland* blew in on the rocks near Bay de Verde. A shift in the wind took the ship off the rocks before she would have broken up. The news of her situation reached the shores of Bay de Verde.

The disaster took place just three years prior to Marconi's wireless radio transmission. This latest development in technology still may not have saved the men if following years of merchants' lack of concern for their workers were an indication. Not long after wireless radios were added to sealing ships, they were removed to save money, a major factor in both the *Southern Cross* and *Newfoundland* disasters.

The bad news of the *Greenland*'s crew reached St. John's when a message was telegraphed from Bay de Verde. Two weeks after departing, the "cursed" ship made her return through the St. John's Narrows and landed her cargo of seals, frozen corpses, and severely frostbitten survivors. Andy Maloney was among the living. The following news clip appeared in the *Daily News* a few days later.

AT THE HOSPITAL
There are only four patients from the Greenland at the hospital now. . . . Andrew Maloney, one of the others, has his ears badly seared.

Maloney stayed alive by taking the clothes off frozen corpses. While Maloney was attempting to remove a coat from what he presumed to be a dead sealer, a weak voice whispered through a mask of ice, "I'm not dead yet."

Andy Maloney lived to be ninety-two.

Muggeridge's Cove, Tickle Cove, with Wester Head in background on left. (Author photo)

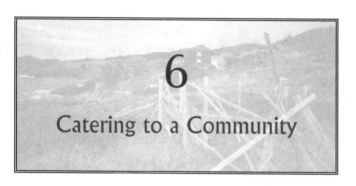

6

Catering to a Community

Mr. Johnny fed people and their horses, too.
Billy Dooley, Plate Cove

IN ORDER TO keep up with the demands of life, over the years, essential provisions were carried and sold by many Tickle Cove storeowners. It was paramount all the right materials were made available, and the best methods applied to ensure an organized, thriving community persevered. In addition to the transaction of business, local stores became important centres for socializing among community neighbours.

The term "planter" referred to a man who employed others to fish from his boat. Entrepreneurs took advantage of what seemed to be an unconditional, bottomless ocean. A "trader" or merchant referred to someone who gave money or supplies in exchange for fish. One such dealer at Tickle Cove during the mid-1800s was David

Candow, a native of Dunkeld, Scotland. He also operated a schooner named the *Swift*. A trader named Angus MacEachern did business at Tickle Cove after Candow.

The rugged harbour defining Tickle Cove was once crowded with timbers comprising stores, stageheads, flakes, and boats. Within the bounds of this plantation, the Ryan Firm of Bonavista supplied dealers such as Joseph, Issac, and John Legge, James and Thomas White, Nicholas Kelly (senior and junior), and Michael Neyle.

Thomas Legge was granted a license to run a bar or "public house" at Tickle Cove in 1873. Fiddler Paddy Mulcahey kept a convenience store near Tickle Cove Pond while another shop was provided by Robert Prince.

At the turn of the twentieth century, Joseph Lane operated a canning business near the brook flowing into Tickle Cove harbour. Both Lane and Bill Kelly kept facilities for refining cod liver oil.

Kept in molasses puncheons and once taken regularly by young and old alike in Newfoundland, cod liver oil contains elongated omega-3 fatty acids which positively affect the lining of the arteries. Vitamins A and D found in the oil help improve muscle function and support the elasticity of blood vessels. Among other functions, cod liver oil is highly recommended to people at risk for heart disease.

Keels merchant John Murphy set up a store at Tickle Cove in 1905. He collected fish in his schooner the *H. F. Wilson*. Murphy also owned and used the schooner *Francis* there from 1876 to 1927. Murphy's branch manager, Dickie White, carried everything "from a needle to an anchor." The firm bought berries from residents in the fall.

The dry goods of Philip Templeman and Company were sold by Joseph Lane at his store while his brother, Charles William, ran a supply trade during the span of 1912–1920. Joseph Legge also ran a "grog" shop. After the first catch of a new fishing season, the fish belonging to the last man to take his catch out of the hold were called "grog fish," leaving him to buy drinks, or grogs, for the rest of the crew.

As is the case of many aspects of rural economy, the above-mentioned businesses failed as a result of dramatic changes in the price of fish, both during and following the First World War.

A man by the name of Frank Kelly also owned and operated a store at Tickle Cove between 1925 and 1930. Kelly also acted as an employment agent for the A.N.D. Company, hiring Tickle Cove men to work in the lumber woods of both Millertown and Badger. He also served time as an agent for the Mutual Life Assurance Company. Kelly, who had accomplished so much in his life, was found dead in Tickle Cove Pond near his home in the spring of 1934.

Smaller stores existed in Tickle Cove throughout the twentieth century, including those belonging to Mathias and Hannah Lane, and Michael and Sarah Connors. The latter family's descendants, Timothy Connors Sr. and Jr., were coopers at Tickle Cove during the first half of the nineteenth century. Lane's small shop housed a downsized pool table which provided a centrepiece for social activity. The Connors family, in business since 1954, remains today with the community's only confectionery store at the bottom of Tickle Cove Pond.

Attempts to mine iron ore, along with reported traces of gold and quartz, were made in the late 1800s, and twice again in the early 1900s. The topic was immortalized in song by Frank Kelly with *Digging for Gold in Otter Gulch Cove*. The rocks of Tickle Cove and surrounding areas are of interest to geologists because of their unique redness which changes to variations of purple throughout the year.

MERCHANTS

No one would have survived in an outport community without the presence of a merchant. Fishermen purchased gear required for a season from the merchant who, in turn, reduced debts owing upon the exchange of fish. Merchants also supplied essential commodities such as flour, salt, peas, beans, and molasses. Such enterprises lost thousands of dollars in this system of trust, known as the "truck" system, while residents, rightfully, pinched every copper. According to those whose lives revolved around merchants, this negative view seems to have somehow side-stepped the Tickle Cove area. The same cannot be said for much of the island.

By far, the most prominent and long-lasting business associated with the people of Tickle Cove was that of the Quintons. Their mercantile endeavours catered to more than twenty communities for more than a century. Those who remember dealing with the Quintons claim they were fair individuals. They say they understood the time and energy needed to keep communities together. After all, when work was put on hold for a get-together, a strong sense of community was necessary to ensure the best possible time. And who was the merchant to get in the way of that, especially when he was right in the middle of it with all the rest?

Red Cliff Island was first settled by Channel Islands brothers William and Andrew Quinton in 1798. In 1806, John Quinton and his brothers, sons of one of the founders, carried on business at the family premises there. The Quintons eventually moved in from the island to an adjacent cove, however the community was referred to as Red Cliff Island into the twentieth century. A next-generation John Quinton, born in 1840, built a shop and a salt store, followed by a post office in the 1870s. In 1872, he married Susanna Mifflin of Bonavista and began a business based on the method of exchanging dried fish for groceries and fishing supplies. The Quinton family residence served as the heart of the business. Constructed by David Marshall in 1884, it remains a strong reminder of the wealth and commerce which once dominated the shoreline.

Following Quinton's death at fifty-three in 1893,

Taking a spell. Raymond Legge, Jim Legge, Ambrose Lane of Tickle Cove, and two unidentified boys watch as Gerald Quinton grades the fish of Plate Cove East brothers Thomas, Leo, and Walter Philpott *circa* 1952. In the background, barrels, each containing 448 lbs. of freshlypacked salmon, are rolled out and ready to go aboard a truck to J. T. Swyers in Bonavista. (Courtesy of Gerald and Hilda Quinton)

Susanna took over the family business and scaled it down. She remained on top of the business until 1917. At this time, upon seeing the need for a more comprehensive general store, the Quintons' sons, John and William, reinvigorated the business. Susanna passed away December 2, 1932, at age seventy-six.

Considered the "outside man," William was responsible for shovelling salt and coal, keeping cattle, culling fish, and overseeing the upkeep of the busy premises.

John, the "inside man," kept business transaction records in order. It was his duty to make sure all essen-

Darrell Duke

In 1939, with the help of Jimmy Fitzgerald of Open Hall, Jimmy Taylor converted Quintons' original one-storey shop into the three-storey structure which still withstands the elements of the sea. The store was first heated by a potbelly stove, then a "Dixie." It is interesting to note the unique method by which the men are about to add walls and floors, raising the roof as they go. (Courtesy of Gerald and Hilda Quinton)

tial commodities were available to the public. For years, his business was second to none in Bonavista Bay. With new stores, stages, and wharves going up all around, "Mr. Johnny," as he was known, bought and exported goods including cod liver oil, dried cod, fresh salmon, seal pelts, and herring. He bought fish cask hoops by the thousands and sold them to other fish merchants around Newfoundland. A fish cask was a fish-storage container made of wooden staves bound by iron or wooden hoops. Hoops, mostly made from birch, were cut by men and carried out of the woods in bundles of twenty-four and sold to the merchant for roughly twenty cents a bundle.

Quintons' customers spanned the farthest reaches of Bonavista Bay. When it was time to restock food and supplies, the father of a family was responsible for going to the merchant. The outside man would take his note and pass it inside, where items such as tea, sugar, fruit, biscuits, peas, and beans were purchased in twenty-pound sacks.

After he graded the fish, the outside man would write the amount and grade on a note and bring it to the skipper in the office, who credited the fisherman in his ledger. When the fishing season was over, the fisherman came and "straightened up" with Mr. Johnny. If money was owed to the fisherman, it was paid then.

Aside from the demands of the mercantile system, John Quinton, Jr. had foxes come from Prince Edward Island. This was the basis of a fox farm he operated at

Red Cliff from 1925 to 1936. It was also the outside man's responsibility to manage the foxes. Bred for their fur, foxes were not considered fit for human consumption. There was one man, however, belonging to Jamestown, Bonavista Bay, who used to eat fox meat. The fox pens may be seen at Red Cliff today as evidence of another successful component of the Quinton family business.

The person employed the longest by the Quintons during their period of business was Jimmy Taylor. Known as a good fisherman and a "great hand to split fish," Taylor went to work for Johnny Quinton in 1926. In addition to being a fine carpenter, he also worked hard at Quintons' cod traps. Although he could not read or write, the small, quiet Tickle Cove man adeptly helped construct much of the business premises. Wearing the same clothes in winter as he did in summer, Taylor was often seen walking to and from Tickle Cove with 100-pound sacks of food on his back. Hard luck fell upon Taylor and his wife, Dorcas, in March 1956, when their twelve-year-old son, Chesley, died of smoke inhalation during a fire which destroyed their Tickle Cove home. The man who could "do it all" worked with John Quinton Limited until 1963. Taylor died in March 1992, six months shy of his one hundredth birthday.

The Quintons bought most of their supplies from James Baird Limited in St. John's, including molasses, a common staple in feeding large families. It came in two containers: "puncheons," large barrels capable of holding between forty-four and 140 gallons of liquid; and a "tierce," a smaller barrel designed to hold roughly forty-two gallons. Too heavy to lift, two men would roll the puncheons to their destination. One time a 100-gallon molasses puncheon got away from its handlers and rolled down over a hill and onto the store bridge, spilling its contents over everything in its path. Gerald Quinton humorously recalls the sight of Jimmy Taylor walking up from the store through the molasses. Aside from the purpose of baking, molasses was in great demand for the making of beer and moonshine, especially in the days of prohibition. When a puncheon was empty, they "sawed 'em off" and used the smaller puncheon tubs for salting fish.

Cod tongues, later considered a Newfoundland delicacy, were only taken when someone wanted a different kind of meal. Although they were not sold by the Quintons, cod tongues provided quick income for young fellows working on the premises during summer months. Because fish was so plentiful at one time, cod heads, tongues and all, were discarded.

When fish was drying, Quintons hired an extra twenty-five to thirty people to ensure the work was done on time. This massive hiring continued for many years. "They took in squid by the thousands. No trouble to get a day's work down there at twenty cents an hour," Captain Russell said.

A train car full of tinned milk often awaited the Quintons at Princeton train station. Piled in the pantry of their home, milk was kept from freezing by the steady heat of a Warm Morning stove. By winter most men had their supplies, and business naturally slowed.

The business of Joseph Thomas Swyers first planted its roots in Bonavista in 1894, but was officially engaged in the fishery business in 1920. It was from there Quintons ordered coal carried by Swyers' schooners the *Isabelle H.* and the *Celtic*. Once unloaded at Open Hall, the slow-burning fuel was carried back to the store and packed away until sold or used.

While others were busy earning meagre wages fishing the Labrador, Johnny Quinton decided to cash in on the scene. But first he needed a boat. A big boat.

The schooner *Molly Fern* was built at Haystack, Placentia Bay, in 1920. The enormous vessel proved a dandy for the long haul northward. Years later, merchant and soon-to-be schooner owner James Baird awaited her arrival through the St. John's Narrows. When he saw the boat, he shouted in joy, "'Tis she! 'Tis she!" From then on, she was called the *Tishy*. The Bairds used the schooner to carry fish to distant markets.

Johnny Quinton purchased the schooner in 1934. She was immediately taken to the Labrador coast by Tickle Cove's John White. White, who had spent most of his life in the lumber woods, had been to the Labrador in a schooner, but never behind the wheel of a boat or under his own command. His nerve is remembered well today by those who knew him. Captain White died in August 1937. From 1935 to 1941, Captain Norman Handcock of Eastport took to the *Tishy*'s helm. Part of the summer of

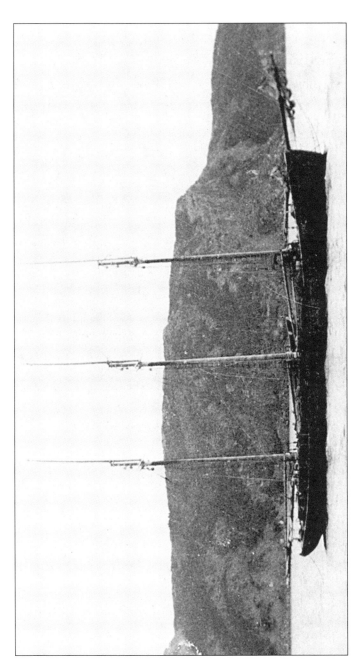

The *Tishy*, in collar here at Open Hall, was purchased by Red Cliff merchant Johnny Quinton in 1934. The schooner was immediately taken to the Labrador by Captain John White of Tickle Cove. (Courtesy of Ron and Jesse Fitzgerald)

1941, while Captain Handcock was ill, both Joe Humby of Summerville and Rex Oldford of Red Cliff skippered her at different times.

Every spring, Quintons geared her up for the long voyage to the Labrador. Nets were mended and twine was dyed dark, or "barked," making nets less visible to fish. Including the cook, skipper, and engineer, the *Tishy* sailed out of port with a crew of seventeen men. Each year, they left the latter part of June and returned in late August or early September, depending on the availability of cod. This ultimately determined the success of the trip. The schooner was equipped with a small engine used mostly when going into ports. When not fishing, the *Tishy* was "coasting" the Labrador coast, delivering supplies as well as carrying junks of wood to St. John's.

Tickle Cove men who served on the *Tishy* included Edward Candow, Michael Lane, John White, Edward White, and Joe Lane. Captain John Russell spent the summers of 1934 and 1935 as mate on her. Open Hall brothers Ron and Bert Fitzgerald, William Gould, Luellen Fitzgerald, and Plate Cove's Jim Russell and Mike Keough served on the schooner as well, among many others.

The *Tishy* was sold to a fisherman in Wesleyville in 1942. The 130-ton vessel was wrecked at Shambler's Cove, Bonavista Bay, in 1950. All crew members survived.

The beloved schooner is immortalized in poetry by Captain John Russell:

TISHY
by Captain John Russell

The *Tishy* was a wooden ship built in Newfoundland.
Built of wooden timbers. Built by local men.
The Master Builder was a man, I've heard the people say.
A self-made man; no doubt was he, from Placentia Bay.

To be a little more precise, there's more I'd like to say.
There's a little place called Haystack up in Placentia Bay.
Where the builder and the *Tishy*, they two first saw the light.
He the Master Builder; The *Tishy*—his delight.

The hull is painted garden green, the deck is painted red.
The spurs are bright with varnish from deck to her mastheads.
They total three in number, and when you look up high,
You can also see three topmasts looming in the sky.

The sails are twelve in number. Their colour snowy white.
Made from snow-white canvas that shows up in the night.
There's the spanker sail and mainsail, the foresail all in trim.
With the jumbo sail, two outer jibs brings *Tishy* to the wind.

Six sails in number now you see, and that is only half.
To see the six that still remain, you have to go aloft.
Three topmast staysails you will see; directly under them
Are three gaff topsails fluttering in the wind.

Now, coming back on deck again, there's lots more you will see.
The cabin house, the steering wheel, the compass—that makes three.
But of all the most important gear, I'm sure you'll understand
are the anchors and the lifeboats when coming to the land.

The pumps, they are important, too, if water you must bail.
Or if the boat is sinking out in a heavy gale.
If the pumps get choked up tight, as they very often do,
you're doomed for "Davey's Locker," yourself and all the crew.

But don't feel sad to what I've said, there is another side.
More bright in its fulfillment in places far and wide.
For if you have a captain and a mate who understand,
and know their navigation, they'll bring you to the land.

There's one more verse I have to write to make it all complete.
The tonnage is 130, width—twenty-seven feet.
The depth is ten feet to the keel, length-feet 102.
Thank you all for listening to the *Tishy*'s interview.

William Quinton died in 1956. Mr. Johnny died in 1965 and was succeeded by William's sons, Gerald and Dolph.

Reminiscing of what "Uncle" Johnny dedicated his life to, Gerald and his wife, Hilda, fondly recall the days when the harbour in front of their home was full of boats while, at times, as many as 150 people stood on the shoreline, each one waiting for his fish to be graded. And with luck, they would not be "in the hole."

Quinton Premises: In 1994, the Heritage Foundation of Newfoundland and Labrador recognized the Quinton Premises as registered heritage structures. (Author photo)

Johnny Quinton was known as a fair and honest man. While people stood around waiting to cash in fish or berries, or to pick up supplies, Quinton often took them into his home and gave them food.

Weaned on the tricks of successful commerce, third-generation businessmen and brothers Gerald and Dolph were seasoned at it all. They remained in business until 1990.

7

Throughout the Year

You are in mortal danger.
Samuel Legge, to a tree he's about to chop down.

W HEN LEARNING OF our forefathers and the hard lives they lived, we find it amazing, sometimes unbelievable. Oblivious of the intensity of everyday chores, men, women, and children each played their roles, morning, noon, and night. Work was carried out free of hesitation, and careful measures were taken every step of the way to ensure nothing had to be repeated. There was no time for mistakes, and less time for laziness. A weak worker in a family could mean the difference between merchantable and West Indies prices for fish. Each family member knew his or her responsibilities from a very early age. There was no nine-to-five or overtime. Mostly it was straight time with little or no pay. In the days when education was not compulsory, fathers took their children out of school to help lessen the burden set upon themselves since they were young.

Although Sundays were long regarded as a day of rest, work continued to some degree in order to maintain consistency. Long breaks in work could very well throw off the flow of the following week's progress. It was everyone's duty to ensure all hands were moving at all times. With such a steady workload consuming their weeks, a good source of energy-providing food was of absolute importance.

A typical breakfast consisted of boiled fresh fish, or salmon, and homemade bread. On Sundays, families had Jiggs' dinner if no fresh (meat) was accessible. On Monday, one might sit down to fish 'n' brewis, fish stew, or soup. Whatever kind of fish was on hand became the choice meal on Wednesdays. Thursday was a time for a change with a lovely feed of fresh chicken, or a saltwater bird such as a turr or a duck. Watered-down salt fish, with potatoes and drawn butter, satisfied the gut on Fridays. Although neither Protestants nor Catholics were permitted to eat meat on Fridays, many fried out fat pork and poured the grease over their fish. A traditional suppertime selection still consumed in parts of the province is leftovers from dinner, with bread and butter.

In November, firewood was cut and piled for hauling by horse and sled when the snow came. Wood from the previous year was burned while new wood was piled to dry. Not everyone had a horse for hauling wood. Men took hand slides, cut their wood, hauled it down to the pond, and took it home across the ice. Some people used goats. In the early days at Tickle Cove, dogs were also used for hauling wood. Snowshoes or "rackets" were carried and worn in places where snow made walking and working unmanageable.

Prepared for a day in the woods, a knapsack contained enough food to cook two meals. Roasted fish and homemade bread were a great means to keep energy levels high. A handful of loose tea, tied in a little brown paper, was put into a boiling kettle, generally a tin can suspended by rabbit wire from a stick over an open fire. When the water started to boil, tea leaves rose to the top. With the stick, the can was raised for a few moments and set down above the fire again. When this process was repeated three times, all tea leaves remained at the bottom. The tea was ready for pouring. Fish and bread washed down with tea made a day in the woods seem as good as a day at home.

The night before heading into the woods, a salted herring was boiled. It was reheated the next day over the open fire, and eaten with slices of homemade bread. When men came out of the woods at night, fish and potatoes, pork fat and onions, and even pea soup provided a lovely supper. Not to mention a fine nap afterwards.

Although children took advantage of rare downtime during summer months, their workload was still of primary importance. Carrying water from the pond was a constant chore, as well as weeding potatoes. Families

Long before all-terrain vehicles, goats were a reliable means of transporting man and wood across frozen ponds. (Courtesy of Fisheries' Library, Department of Fisheries and Oceans)

ensured enough barrels of water were on hand to last the long winter ahead. Aside from storing water, barrels were used for storing nets. Once cut in half, they were used as wash tubs.

After the hay was cut, it was spread to dry. Then it was piled into heaps. Men took these heaps home on their backs and family members fed hay to cattle and other livestock as necessary.

Almost every family kept one or two pigs. A young pig was purchased around September, and stall-fed, as the expression goes. The next fall, it was killed for food.

The main sources of a pig's diet were caplin, dogfish, and just about anything else put in front of it. Rowing outside the Arch Island, boys would "throw away the anchor," heave out their lines, and catch boat-loads of dogfish for this purpose. When they reached the shore, they cut open the dogfish, removing the liver and throwing it into empty beef barrels. The dogfish itself was dried before it was fed to the pigs. After a week, sometimes two, the livers rotted and oil rose to the top while the dregs sank to the bottom. Most times, adults removed the oil, or "dipped it off."

Dogfish liver oil, much like cod liver oil, was in great demand. It sold for twenty-five to thirty cents a gallon. After fifteen or twenty gallons were collected, it was sold or traded to Johnny Quinton for its worth in such items as a cake of soap, a pound of biscuits, or a couple of reels of thread.

In June, caplin were gathered by the thousands, salted

and fed to pigs. A family had to dry ten to twelve barrels of caplin for winter pig feed. "The fatter the better" was the order of the day for the pigs. Growing to at least 200 pounds, pigs were a blessing. Fresh pork was worth the effort it took to keep the animal. When it came time for sports, a pig's bladder proved to be a great substitute for a soccer ball.

Some kept goats to both eat and sell. Its meat is similar in taste to that of deer. People also kept sheep for food. Its greasy, wooly taste was enough to keep some at a distance, but for the most part it was enjoyed.

In addition to keeping sheep for food, its wool was an excellent source for the making of homemade quilts, a staple of the traditional Newfoundland household. One woman held a sheep while another, using a knife or scissors, cut off the wool. The wool was carded by stringing it around the four legs of an upturned chair. Then it was washed out and hung on fences to dry. Most clothing items were knitted by women. In their spare time, especially during winter months, women hooked mats. A brin bag sewn into a frame served as a canvas for the craft.

Most animals were "let go" in the summer and rounded up in the fall. Sometimes this chore took a week. The odd time, a horse or cow got stuck in the bog and perished. Once an animal's time had run its course, it was killed for food. Its fat was saved and mixed with lye to make soap. This process took place in a fire near the home. Soap was cut into square cakes and spared along.

Most times, meat, such as goat, and beef, was exported outside the province by farmers and in turn bought back by Newfoundland merchants who sold it to locals. On the mainland, beef was preserved in brine to ensure it did not spoil. Salt beef, though it is a great catalyst for the onset of high blood pressure and heart disease, remains a delicacy in the province.

Residents of Tickle Cove shared with one another in times of need. If someone killed a pig or a sheep, it was not uncommon for them to give a quarter to their neighbour.

During the first quarter of the twentieth century, a barrel of beef cost anywhere from eighteen to twenty dollars. With roughly 200 pounds of beef in a barrel, and often as much as thirty extra pounds, it was common for a couple of families to buy a barrel of beef between them at the wholesale price. The extra beef was taken out and divided. This practice saved a lot of money and provided many extra meals.

Modernization has provided us with a world full of pointless accessories. Life's essentials have become camouflaged through overexposure to commercialism. This has shaped many ideals as to what a family really needs to survive. Years ago, in the absence of television ads, billboards, and Internet popups, materialism never stood a chance at financially disarming a household. Hard-earned money was spent only as needed, not as desired. For example, in 1931, a bed, a 200-pound barrel of beef, a thirty-two-pound tub of butter, a 100-pound sack of peas, and a 100-pound sack of beans could be purchased at St. John's for thirty-two dollars. If one could afford to get there, it was well worth the trip. There was no time for leisurely stopovers. The absence of distractions such as government's video gambling machines and fast food outlets helped families in ways unimaginable.

The people of Tickle Cove helped each other in more ways than sharing food. If a house needed shingling, all available men joined in to help. If a boat had to be hauled from the water, all hands pitched in to get the job done. Tickle Cove native Captain John Russell remembers how his community's people answered when the time came to help.

"They were friendly. They'd give you the last thing they had . . . . If they had it and you wanted it, you had it, and vice versa. Everybody was alike. If the trawl fishery was not so good due to stormy weather, or lack of bait when squids were scarce, if somebody was luckier than you and they got more fish than they needed for the winter, if your potato crop was bad for the fall and you didn't have potatoes enough for the winter, and somebody else had more than you, you wouldn't do without. That was it! Give! Give! Give!"

People made their money in the summer. In the fall they bought what they needed to survive the winter. A pound of cheese could be purchased for twenty-five cents, while a pound of salt beef cost fifty to sixty cents. A case of milk cost about five dollars. All vegetables were grown.

Caplin was wheeled in a barrow and dumped as fertilizer on potato beds. Cod heads provided nutrients for turnip and cabbage.

Once September struck, potatoes were dug from the ground and put away. October saw the extraction, cleaning, and storing of cabbage, turnip, carrots, and other root vegetables people were lucky enough to grow. These were sown in June month.

Amidst the barrage of constant work throughout the year, people made a point to visit each other at night. During a game of cards and a few drinks, someone had to sing a song, a must-do pastime of years gone by. This practice was never more evident than during the Christmas season. November and most of December were spent in preparation for the well-deserved break which lay ahead.

PREPARING FOR FATHER CHRISTMAS

When discussing calender events, it is always useful to be aware of their origins. That way we become more in tune with the moment of discussion by feeling part of the past. Most times we feel history is make-believe because it happened so long ago. Change, being inevitable, allows us to see ourselves as part of the making of a particular history.

Winter solstice, or "sun standing still," was tradition-ally celebrated on December 20, 21, or 22. This night, known by the Romans as the ceremony of *Saturnalia*, was regarded by pagans as the night which Great Mother Goddess gave birth to a new sun, in turn restarting the cycle of the four seasons.

In the year AD 274 Roman Emperor Aurelian proclaimed December 25 *Natalis Solis Invicti*: the festival of the birth of the invincible sun. In AD 320 Pope Julius I specified December 25 as the official birth date of Jesus Christ. Five years later, the first Christian Roman Emperor, Constantine the Great, changed the solstice celebrations into the Mass of Christ, or Christmas.

Santa Claus, to whom we are accustomed today, derived from the charitable customs of Saint Nicholas (AD 270–310), the Bishop of Myra (Myra now part of modern-day Turkey). Later regarded as the Patron Saint of Children, Nicholas was often seen riding on a donkey, dressed in a bishop's red-and-white robe, giving gifts to children. When Saint "Nick" died, his remains were enshrined in a church in the Italian city of Bari. Legend suggests the first crusaders visited the shrine and carried his stories abroad. The anniversary of his death, December 6, became a day to exchange gifts in his honour.

The celebration of *Sinterklaas*, or Santa Claus, was first introduced to North America by the Dutch who founded New Amsterdam, later renamed New York upon colonization by the British. In 1822, poet and theology professor Clement Clark Moore published the poem *A Visit From St. Nicholas*, better known as *The Night Before*

Christmas, taken from the poem's opening line. In his words, Moore vividly depicts a description of St. Nick, and eight tiny reindeer, each with their own name. He even conjured up the notion of the gift giver returning by way of the chimney.

In 1885, Boston printer Louis Prang first introduced Christmas cards depicting the ever-changing image of St. Nick with gifts to shower all. In an effort to boost sales of their product in the 1930s, Coca-Cola hired illustrator Haddon Sunblom to create the jolly, white-bearded character we know as Santa Claus today. Up to that point in Newfoundland, "Father Christmas" was the one children hoped to catch a glimpse of on Christmas Eve. Rum and cake, left as an offering, occupied the kitchen tables of homes with anxious children pretending to be asleep upstairs in their hay-strewn beds. Crumbs and an empty glass on the table in the morning confirmed the old man was satisfied.

By far the most special and unique tradition in Newfoundland is Christmas. Every corner of the island contains its own way of celebrating, one never far removed from the other. Because it was so special, a lot of things were "put back" on account of Christmas.

During Christmas at Tickle Cove, people made up for a hard year's work in memorable style. In the olden days, Christmas was celebrated to its fullest degree as a result of strong will, hard work, and flawless timing. Unmindful of lights and trimmed trees, pleasant anticipation filled the hearts of every generation.

All work was done by four o'clock Christmas Eve. A month before Christmas, grandmothers, mothers and daughters, baked raisin bread and stored it in cellars for freshness. Mummers quietly plotted what they were going to wear during the traditional visits. Countless loaves of bread were baked while enough wood to last two weeks was cut, split, and piled. Men were busy making homebrew. If it was not strong enough, they steamed it into a face-distorting drop of moonshine. Gallons of black currant, blueberry, and dogberry wine waited in seasoning for folks preparing for the special days ahead. No work was done during the twelve days of Christmas. Rita Tremblett recalls her grandfather, Captain John White, saying to his grandchildren, "Youms got to get ready for Father Christmas."

Two days before Christmas, the kitchen floor was tarred and pitched. With sand swept about the floor, pot liquor was thrown over it. After another dose of sand, the floor was swept, leaving a perfect shine. Now they were ready for a time.

When four o'clock struck in some homes on Christmas Eve, bottles were placed on tables and shot glasses were tipped back for the first of many straight holiday drinks. At five o'clock, a pot of watered, dry cod fish was cooked and served with homemade figgie bread. Cocoa warmed the bellies of children.

After supper on Christmas Eve, several Catholic men from the three communities walked to and from Midnight Mass in King's Cove; twelve miles from Tickle Cove. Each had his own flask of rum, whiskey, or 'shine' to keep him warm. As times progressed, they hired a truck for the trip and all hands piled in the back. Most went to church on Christmas morning.

Many stayed up all night visiting relatives and friends engaging in the high-spirited square dance. To the last house, each man brought a share of mutton or beef to be included in the big scoff at midnight. With cabbage and potatoes, the meal was enjoyed to the fullest. Standing in a circle and holding hands, young and old alike danced to their favourite songs. With windows and doors wide open, and the stove red hot, accordions and fiddles brought in the peaceful tune of Christmas morning in a hurry.

If the crowd had to leave the last house earlier than anticipated, those willing to stay up often used someone's shed as a stand-in for a kitchen and would 'plank 'er down' until daylight. When they got home, a drop of homemade soup did wonders for self-inflicted illnesses. If that failed to do the trick, a nap on the kitchen settle or 'daybed' before going to church helped to meet the body's requirements. Christmas dinner treated the hangover until the next spurt of fun began. The process continued for twelve days.

Christmas was the time of year when people focused on togetherness instead of the sometimes-difficult balance of give and take expected during the season today. Father Christmas left an apple or an orange for each child. Sometimes he left a piece of sweet bread; the only time of year many got to taste the delicious homemade treat. A popular candy given at Christmas in the olden days was Gibraltar, the oval-shaped, green-with-red-striped candy. Everything was appreciated. The only thing adults exchanged were dancing partners and pats on the back, all in the name of a closely-knit community.

Candlemass Day was celebrated on February 2. Mothers dripped candle wax in the shape of the holy cross into the left shoes or boots of her family members. No breakfast was had until this ritual was over.

A general consensus exists amongst Tickle Cove's eldest today: Christmas is not like it was.

Tickle Cove Pond

Most famous as the result of a folk ballad by Mark Walker, *Tickle Cove Pond* has become well-known to hundreds of people for generations. The waters of the pond originate on the back of Keels. Nestled in a valley below Queen's Hill at Keels is Squib Cove Pond. Although it has always been referred by area folk as Squid's Cove Pond, the surname Squib once existed at Keels. Squib Cove Pond runs into Rocky Pond which, in turn, flows into Birchy Pond. Brothers Roland and Jim Russell used to keep a small rowboat in Rocky Pond providing a shorter, more enjoyable trip across the water to bakeapple marshes on the other side. From Birchy Pond, waters meander in brooks through wilderness until quenching the banks of Fisher's Pond, ultimately making their way to Tickle Cove Pond. Tickle Cove Pond empties its waters through a brook on the beach and into the Atlantic Ocean.

The waters from Squib Cove Pond to Tickle Cove Pond span a distance of approximately six miles. Tickle Cove Pond measures approximately three quarters of a mile in length, and about a quarter-mile in width.

Across the beach and over the Big Hill, there is a series of gardens known as the Pond Gardens. Stretching alongside the pond, the gardens were once crowded with vegetables, cattle, and haystacks. Almost every family in Tickle Cove used a piece of land here. Many years ago, the gardens were also the site of annual garden parties where people played dice, shot for the bulls-eye with air guns, and spun the wheel of fortune for baking pans and teapots.

Bakeapples were picked in August while other berries were gathered in the fall. Just three miles inside Tickle Cove were two popular berry-filled marshes called Russell's Marsh and the peculiarly named bog Tumble Down Dick. Thousands and thousands of bakeapples and other berries were carried home from these areas. At fifteen cents a gallon, partridgeberries were sold to Mr. Johnny who, in turn, shipped them in barrels.

Blueberries, for the most part, were kept for baking homemade pies, buns, cakes and other desserts. Berries were picked in summer and fall to provide enough jam to last an entire year.

Tickle Cove Pond is also cherished for its annual dory races. Although the races' date of origin is unknown, the event is said to have been started by a local parish priest, Father Murphy. The names of all the crew of the 1939 Tickle Cove team have vanished in the annals of time, but thanks to surviving 1939 Red Cliff champion Jim Oldford, the names of his teammates and coxwain are recalled. Pulling for coxswain Fred Oldford in the four-oared, eighteen-foot boat were the crew of Gus Oldford, Jim Oldford, Gus Randell, and Joe Bowen. The crew's first-place prize was a suit of oil clothes, which they sold, splitting the profits. Crew members Gus Oldford and Gus Randell died overseas during the Second World War.

The races were revived as part of Open Hall-Red Cliff-Tickle Cove Come Home Year's agenda in 1997. This time around, eighty-four-year-old Jim Oldford took to the rudder as coxswain and steered his team to victory. Prior to 1997, folks recall, the last race was held in 1939.

Proof the races existed earlier comes in the form of song. *The Races on Tickle Cove Pond*, credited to Mark Walker, provides an interesting insight into the event. In 1865, Newfoundland switched from pounds, shillings, and pence to the North American standard of the decimal currency. The reference to currency in the lyrics indicates the song was written before 1865. The number of races between the 1860s and 1939, however, is unknown.

THE RACES ON TICKLE COVE POND
by Mark Walker

John Kelly the builder, a man of great skill—
He built a fine boat for himself and young Bill.
He called her the *Shamrock*, she looked good and strong.
Brought "Jackie the Shiner" down Tickle Cove Pond.

Sam Prince "the Buck" built another fine boat.
Oh boys, what a dandy when she goes afloat.
The crowd they all viewed her as they passed along.
Saying, "Row you two buckos" on Tickle Cove Pond.

'Twas early next morning two owners came down.
John Kelly to Sam'l, "I'll bet twenty pounds."
"Here's twenty," says Sam'l, "Pounds, shillings and pence."
With that, the two owners sat back on the fence.

The signal for starting was the firing of guns.
The flags were a-waving and beating of drums.
They kept even turns and they kept even strokes.
But, the *Shamrock* was leading and rounding the post.

"Three cheers for the *Shamrock*," cried out Honer Gale.
"Hip, hip, hoorah!" cried out Tommy Neal.
"Foul play," said Ned Humby, "for I broke an oar.
"But I'll have satisfaction when I gets on shore."

Very soon after the boat struck the beach.
Bill Walker stepped forward, our heroes to meet.
They were eager for battle, so at it they went.
And they mangled each other to their hearts' content.

In the middle of the fight, Dick Quinton stepped in.
There was Harry and Copper and Aunt Grace's Jim.
There were Taylors and Humbys and Princes and Gales;
Candows and Crosss and six of the Neals.

Tickle Cove Pond from the roadside. (Author photo)

The pond, which once offered an endless supply of
brown trout, was also a typical summer site for swimming
and boating. Taking a month longer to warm up than fresh
water, the saltwater coves between Red Cliff and Tickle
Cove were popular swimming spots as well. According to
the doctor, no one was allowed in the ocean until the first
of August. He told children there was poison in the water.
When the time came, rain or shine, children made for the

ocean. Whenever there was a sign of a break in work, back to the pond and beaches they went.

During the winter months, the ice on Tickle Cove Pond provided a natural shortcut for hauling wood. Ice-fishing, hockey (with frozen horse manure serving as a puck), and skating were carried on from one end of the pond to the other. Mrs. Gertrude Maloney, ninety-three, recalls skating on Tickle Cove Pond "in the days when skates were attached to your boots by a screw at the heel." Her Grandfather, Jim Lane, made her a slide which she pushed around the ice while skating. Sliding took place all over the Pond Gardens, as well as on Old Gerald's Hill, located on the opposite side of Tickle Cove Pond.

The waters of Tickle Cove Pond empty through this brook into a harbour once laden with stores, wharves, stages, and boats. (Author photo)

Today, Tickle Cove Pond is as beautiful as ever, serving as a mirror for the sun, clouds, and perimeter houses, some aging over 150 years.

Tickle Cove's only remaining fish stage with Arch Island in the background. (Author photo)

8

Taking Time to Forget

*Sure the youngsters don't go outdoors now. Years ago,
it was a job to get 'em to come in and get something to
eat, afraid they wouldn't get out no more the day. Now,
you almost got to kick 'em out like the cats. The cats
would be gone all night long. Now, you can't go to bed
until the cat comes home.*

Theresa White, telling it like it is.

W HEN CONSIDERING THE stereotypes used to describe the
"carefree, rough-edged" Irish and the "somewhat-
snobby, dry-witted" English comprising our ancestry, it
appears quite contradictory in the face of an outport
house party. Folks of varying religions and ethnic
origins enlisted as one for both the preparation and
execution of a time.

When it came time to tie up the boats, throw down
the pick and shovel, and to forget about the following

week's work, men and women of Tickle Cove covered all angles of groundwork. Every Saturday night was the same. Who would make the soup? Who would contact the fiddle and accordion players? By the time the mats were taken up off the floor, the news of a time spread like wildfire throughout the three communities. By daybreak of the next morning, floors were buckled and feet were tired and sore. After dancing all night, people walked home. There were no cars, let alone taxis, in the days when songs were composed and sung on the spot. Red Cliff's Gerald Quinton remembers the inhabitants of Tickle Cove as "really sporty people who used to have great parties."

Usually the first song of an old-fashioned square dance was "Off She Goes." The partners met and the girl went first and swung around. Next was "Change and Take Two" where a man took two women, one on either side, and "danced 'er up." Then he swung around while another man took both women.

Popular dances included the Lancers, the Reel, and the always popular Kissin' Dance, usually the last dance whereby a man put a cloth over the face of a woman and kissed her to the dance floor. The woman, in turn, took the cloth and kissed another man. The process continued until everyone was out on the floor. As interesting as this may sound, it probably would not go over very well today.

When playing for dances held in community centres, a musician was paid two dollars and fifty cents, plus his supper. The reels began at eight o'clock in the evening and dancing continued throughout the night, until five or six o'clock the next morning.

In later years, at house parties, people paid five dollars to "join the ball." Every man needed a woman for this. For their contribution, they received dinner and booze. The "Big House" in Open Hall was famous for its great parties. The two-family home was owned by three Murphy brothers: Jim and John in one end, and Charlie and his wife in the other. Because it had the most room, it was the "place to go." Sometimes the party went on for two days. After dancing all night, they lay down for a nap, just long enough to get sufficient energy to go at it again.

Tickle Cove produced its fair share of talented musicians, songsters, and singers who catered to kitchen parties and community square dances. Andy Maloney, beyond the nightmare of the *Greenland* disaster, was recognized for his ability to play the violin, or fiddle as it is more commonly known in traditional music. Those who had the privilege of being in his musical presence never heard him complain about his traumatic experiences as a sealer, except for the odd mention of a tired shoulder, which had been frostbitten in the ordeal.

Maloney's home was a place where folks of all ages dropped in at night to hear fine "chunes" from his fiddle. Many young fellows learned to play the instrument by watching him pass the time with his music. The late Mary Mullowney was married to Maloney's son, Jim. She fondly reflected upon the wonderful company and entertainment her father-in-law provided at their home. With no televisions or radio, kitchen music helped pass many long, cold winter nights. Gerald Quinton, a musician himself, recalls visiting Maloney's with his friends. Maloney's sons, Andy and Jim, often sang and danced to the accompaniment of their father. Andy Maloney took a stroke while playing for a party in his kitchen. He died just days later.

The home of Paddy Mulcahey was another popular place to hear great music. Mulcahey, along with his son, Tommy, played duelling fiddles all night long. A favourite tune of theirs was "Tidley Wink the Barber."

Entertainers from other communities also participated soulfully in regular social events. These included Bill Hobbs and Mike Keough of Plate Cove, and Larry Barker, Mary Catherine Barker, and Ron Fitzgerald of Open Hall. Mrs. Barker, recalled for having a lovely voice, is remembered for her renditions of "The Star of Logy Bay," "The Bonavista Line," and "The Ryans and the Pittmans," more commonly known as "We'll Rant and We'll Roar" (like true Newfoundlanders).

VERSES OF THE HEART

The manner in which early Newfoundland songwriters chose tunes for their songs has been evident in all genres of music for the better part of the twentieth century. It has

The kitchen of Paddy and Tommy Mulcahey in Tickle Cove, a place where the sound of music was heard on a regular basis. The almost 150-year-old house near Tickle Cove Pond has been the home of Theresa, and the late Edward White, for more than forty years. (Author photo)

certainly carried over into this new century as well. Mostly, they used the tune from an already popular song. This method is not demeaning in any sense when one reads or hears the crafty manner in which words were cultivated and songs performed.

By far the most popular lyricist of Tickle Cove, and one of Newfoundland's songwriting pioneers, is Mark Walker. Born at Tickle Cove in 1846, to Marcus Walker of County Tipperary, Ireland, and Jane Mackey of Bonavista, Walker was adept at piecing words together in the name of song. He had three brothers, William, John, and Sam, and three sisters, Eliza, Sarah, and Catherine.

Walker worked at the Bennett family mine at Tilt Cove, White Bay. In 1873, he married Mary Downey of Coachman's Cove, Green Bay. They had five children; William, Mark, John, Catherine, and Mary Margaret. Mark Jr. drowned while fishing on the Labrador.

In 1875, along with his brothers, Walker moved from Tickle Cove to Sweet Bay and worked for the Ryan Firm cutting sticks. He was postmaster there in 1888. Records indicate Walker built a schooner named *Speedwell* at Sweet Bay in 1898 for a John Moss.

In boats built by their own hands, the Walker brothers fished the Newfoundland coast, as well as the Labrador. In 1906, Walker and his family moved to Everett, Massachusetts, where he worked as a carpenter. His brother William and his family travelled with them. Soon after, their brother Sam moved there as well, where he worked as a foreman in the cement business. The

Walker family suffered a tragedy when Sam's son, Sam, Jr., was killed in a motorcycle accident. Mark Walker died at Everett in 1928, and is buried at Holy Cross Cemetery in Malden, Massachusetts.

Aside from the traditional classics, "Tickle Cove Pond" and "Fanny's Harbour Bawn," Mark Walker wrote *The Antis of Plate Cove, Nellie Neil (Me Little Kettle), The Races on Tickle Cove Pond, The Girls of Sweet Bay, Labrador Squalls, Lovely Kitty-Oh,* or *Lovely Katie-Oh,* and a second *Tickle Cove Pond.*

Tickle Cove Pond, whose melody stems from the Irish tune "Tatter Jack Walsh," has been performed and recorded by several Newfoundland artists including John White (1965) and Ron Hynes (1991). The latter interpretation brought the song back to life for newer generations of traditional music loyalists. Produced by Kelly Russell and Don Walsh for their album *Another Time,* Hynes delivers the song with caution and respect.

TICKLE COVE POND
by Mark Walker

In cuttin' and haulin', in frost and in snow,
We're up against troubles that few people know.
And it's only by courage and patience and grit,
And eatin' plain food can we keep ourselves fit.

The hard and the easy we take as it comes,
And when ponds freeze over, we shorten our runs.

To hurry me hauling, the spring comin' on,
Near lost me a mare out on Tickle Cove Pond.

Lay hold William Oldford, lay hold William White,
Lay hold of the cordage and pull all your might.
Lay hold of the bowline and pull all you can,
And give me a lift with poor Kit on the pond.

I knew that the ice became weaker each day,
But still took the risk and kept haulin' away.
One evening in April bound home with a load,
The mare showed some halting against the ice road.

And knew more than I did as matters turned out,
And lucky for me had I joined her in doubt.
She turned 'round her head and with tears in her eyes,
As if she were saying, "You're risking our lives."

All this I ignored with a whip handle blow,
For, man is too stupid, dumb creatures to know.
The very next minute the pond gave a sigh,
And down to our necks went poor Kitty and I.

For if I had taken wise Kitty's advice,
I never would take the shortcut on the ice.
Poor creature she's dead, poor creature she's gone,
I'll ne'er get me mare out of Tickle Cove Pond.

So, I raised an alarm you could hear for a mile,

And neighbours turned up in a very short while.
You can always rely on the Oldfords and Whites,
To render assistance in all your bad plights.

To help a poor neighbour is part of their lives,
The same I can say for their children and wives.
When the bowline was fastened around the mare's breast,
William White for a shanty song made a request.

With no time for thinking, no time for delay,
Straight from his head came this song right away.

Lay hold William Oldford, lay hold William White,
Lay hold of the cordage and pull all your might.
Lay hold of the bowline and pull all you can,
And give me a lift with poor Kit on the pond.

Walker is unofficially credited as author of *Down by Jim Long's Stage*, and a suspect in the penning of *The Star of Logy Bay*.

From the generation following Mark Walker's time at Tickle Cove came a talented man named Frank Kelly who owned the first gramophone in Tickle Cove. Kelly was quite popular and willing to share the modern invention with all. Every Sunday evening, the road between Tickle Cove and Red Cliff came alive with young people coming to hear songs from Kelly's record player, which he placed under a cliff.

Aside from writing articles for both the *Daily News* and the *Evening Telegram*, Kelly was known as "a great hand to make up songs, and a wonderful poet." Although it was never published, Kelly pieced together an original collection entitled *Frank Kelly's Peerless Songbook*. The following is an example of his humorous approach to songwriting:

TOMMY LEGGE'S RUM
by Frank Kelly

Come all ye good people I pray pay attention,
Unto these few lines which I'll write for you now.
If you'll pay attention the truth I will mention,
The action which led to the Tickle Cove row.

The fifteenth of August the night had been cloudy,
Determined for action in trouble begun.
Four chaps got together out under the weather,
They made up a plan to steal Tommy Legge's rum.

They came to a place in the centre of the harbour,
Where houses were few and the billows did roar.
Till one chap amongst them got rather faint-hearted,
Lay down for a rest near poor Dickie's shop door.

The other three chaps went, their hands in their pockets,
Determinedly on to the scene of the fun.
Determined that those who had backed out of action
Should never be given a taste of the rum.

They marched up by fences and corners and gateways,
On the tips of their toes so mute as a mouse.
When to their surprise there loomed up before them,
The Legges all in bed, not a light in their house.

Everything in their favour, the moon had just clouded,
They reached for the knob—to get in they were sure.
When to their surprise, they were strucken dumbfounded,
Tommy Legge, his cap off, shoved his head through the door.

Tommy Legge seized his rum, two jars and a bottle,
No coat on his arm and no cap on his head.
Went up to his house in the heck of a hurry,
He beat it upstairs, hid it under his bed.

Many tricks have been done this year in the harbour,
They hung up the dogfish and broomed Paddy's store.
They are through with the game; Tommy Legge can rest easy,
And make all he can and be troubled no more.

A victim of polio, Kelly had a serious limp and used a cane in the summer and a homemade sled to get around in the winter. His life ended tragically on the morning of April 12, 1934, when he and his sled went through the ice on Tickle Cove Pond. Although his death was reported as a drowning, a severe gash in his forehead suggests he struck his head and may have died as a result of the blow.

Frank Kelly's story hardly ends here. A premonition of his death has remained at the forefront of folklore in Tickle Cove.

Another character by the name of Jim Legge once graced Tickle Cove with his "on-the-spot" parodies of local happenings. Among the most talked-about of his creations are *Isaac John's Buck* and *The Moonshine Song*. When people describe Legge's songwriting, they say, "He told it all." If he saw anything funny or strange happening in the community, he remembered it and wrote his own version. The following is an excerpt from Legge's *Isaac John's Buck*:

> When Isaac John heard that his buck was astray,
> 'Twas down to Keels' harbour he went the next day.
> He went to Jim Penny with courage and pluck
> Sayin', "Who give you orders to murder me buck?"

Not too many were shy about belting a song out of them at the height of a time. It almost always ran in families. Annie Kelly, ninety-four, used to love to sing. Others remember her mother, Ann, being "a great lady to sing a song" as well.

B*AYO*

During the summer of 1984, Tickle Cove became the desired location for the filming of the made-for-television movie *Bayo* starring Patricia Phillips, Stephen McGrath, and the late Ed McNamara.

McNamara, known for his roles in films such as *Margin for Error* with Milton Berle, and *The Black Stallion* with Mickey Rooney, played a displaced sea captain who returned to Tickle Cove to spend his dying days with his daughter, played by Phillips, and her illegitimate son, Bayo, played by McGrath.

Phillips is known for her role in the Leonard Nimoy–directed film *The Good Mother*, with Diane Keaton and Liam Neeson. The young McGrath, virtually unheard of at the time, continues to make a living in the Canadian theatre scene.

The movie, produced by Canadian filmmaker and poet Colin Browne, also features locals including Lloyd Oldford of Red Cliff, and the late Paddy Lane of Tickle Cove. Oldford plays the lover of Bayo's mother while Lane plays a quiet old man who ventures in and out of various scenes. Ultimately, he plays the role of a corpse after he is found dead on the ground by local boys playing ball.

Tickle Cove provided an attractive backdrop for the film, which monopolized activity in the community for three weeks. The house the film was shot in belonged to Roland and Jim Russell who, at the time, were using their old home as a fishing outlet for the summer months.

Molly Legge papered the walls of two upstairs bedrooms, as well as the house's front room. The crew borrowed the Legges' old-fashioned enterprise stove for the duration of the shoot.

The shed, which served as the old man's home on Red Cliff Island, as well as some props, were obtained from Harris and Brenda Lodge of Catalina.

Live entertainment on the set was provided by Gerald Quinton and Will Tremblett. The movie's musical score was written by Manitoba-born Loreena McKennitt.

At the end of Tickle Cove is the old house formerly owned by brothers Roland and Jim Russell. In 1984, the house served as the main location for the filming of the movie *Bayo*. Today it is used as a summer residence. (Author photo)

Although *Bayo* was not a blockbuster movie, it did wonders for the community's tourism in the years to follow.

9
Dismantled by Mother Nature

Not a sound was heard. They were better off.
    Gertrude Maloney, on the 1921 tidal surge

ISLANDS HAVE ALWAYS been subjected to freak storms. In 1775, the sea around Newfoundland rose twenty feet above its normal level, and hundreds of boats were destroyed while 300 lives were taken. On September 19, 1846, a tragedy of equal proportion walloped the island. St. Thomas's Church in St. John's was moved bodily, while damage to the city reached $2,000,000.

During the period of October 28–31, 1921, much of Newfoundland's coast was devastated by a tremendous storm. The following article with the headline "Storm Ravages Bonavista Bay" appeared on the front page of the *Evening Advocate* just days later.

Bonavista Bay got her share of buffeting by the

big wind and sea storm—and in more than one place in the Bay today there are to be seen evidences of the havoc wrought by the storm king. Probably not a cove in the historic arm of water was left untouched by the gale. . . . Keels, King's Cove, Amherst Cove, and Stock Cove are reported to the Marine Department as having been swept clean. Stages, wharves, boats, barrels, and all the properties . . . usually to be found along a waterfront—all went before the rages of tide and wind.

Although unspecified in the above-mentioned article, Tickle Cove may have been among the most badly affected communities on the island. The desolation and distress left behind altered the course of the community forever.

The evening of October 30, 1921, began with misty rain. A light northwest wind developed into a major storm overnight. When the people of Tickle Cove went to bed that night, clatters outside their windows seemed no greater than what a lifetime of storms had already produced. There was no foreshadowing to indicate what met their eyes the next morning. As they slept, a sadistic act of nature took place without disturbing the slumber of a single soul.

A tidal surge of enormous magnitude quietly lifted and carried every boat, wharf, stage, and store to the upper end of Tickle Cove Pond. What did not remain on

The vulnerability of Tickle Cove's harbour to the open sea is evident here. With no natural breakwater, it is easy to imagine the impact the tidal surge had upon the harbour and its contents. (Courtesy of Mike and Marge O'Shea)

the pond side of the beach washed out to sea when the water receded. The only structure left standing near the beach was John White's house. Their bread and butter was taken without explanation or remorse.

The "tidal wave," as the event is referred to locally, ruined many gardens and drowned several pigs, cows, and sheep kept for food. People were frightened the sea would return for the scraps it had left behind.

On the night of the tidal wave, eight-year-old Annie Kelly, her sister, and her mother stayed at her grandmother's house for company. Outside in the morning, their two-storey home was sitting by the gate of their grandmother's front fence. The sea lifted the house from its posts, carrying it 200 feet. To their astonishment, and to the credibility of good handiwork, the house was safe and sound. The oil lamp in the kitchen was hanging on its wall bracket, as they had left it. The family also lost a pig in the flood, a devastating blow to the family's food supply. However, they were lucky to have their lives.

Dickie White's two-storey branch office and store took the brunt of the sea due to its location in the middle of the beach. It was carried up the pond with everything else. Puncheons of molasses and barrels of beef, pork, and flour were among a long list of items stolen by the storm. Bill White's liver factory was taken by the sea as well.

When Gertrude Maloney moved to Tickle Cove from Sydney, Nova Scotia, she asked her grandmother, Elizabeth Lane, who owned the old house on the rocks near the harbour. "My Dear, das Mark Walker's," she said. "One of these days das gonna blow down." Walker had left Tickle Cove decades before, leaving his house to fend for itself against the elements of nature. Years of wind, sleet, rain, and snow were no contest for the single swell which engulfed the harbour that night. Grandmother Lane was right. The house was nowhere to be seen the next morning.

Farther down the shore toward Wester Head, two wharves belonging to the Muggridges and Russells were flattened. Back in the harbour, boats, flakes, and stage-heads were smashed to splinters, leaving families in a state of turmoil and disbelief. Boats coming to rest onshore were nothing more than paltry shells, mostly beyond repair. Generations of hard work, and the sole means to a humble livelihood, vanished with a single, unannounced gust of natural hatred. The entire harbour, once lined with evidence of a surviving fishery, was hastily restored to its original state: rocks and water.

Lost were cod traps, herring nets, and lobster cages. In a store by the waterside lay 6,000 pounds of dried cod ready for the market. This, in addition to a new twenty-five-foot motorboat and a five-horsepower Acadia engine, was just more debris left by Mother Nature.

Two of the harbour's pigs taken out to sea returned unharmed to the beach at Red Cliff, still in their pen. Fred Oldford was walking up the road feeling disappointed after losing a pig when he met his curly-tailed friend strolling toward him. The theory that pigs can't swim because they'd cut their throats with their hooves was challenged and crushed that night.

Johnny Quinton also suffered a great loss at Red Cliff during the storm. This brought about major setbacks for the people of Tickle Cove dependent on the merchant for life's necessities. Unfortunately, in this case, help and compensation were scarce, leaving everyone to fend for themselves in the best ways they could.

Remarkably, there was no loss of human life in the Tickle Cove area. The same could not be said for a large portion of the island. As fortunate as people were in this light, most were still left without a trace of the back-breaking toil they slaved for all their lives. Some families tried to piece their lives back together, but their efforts were in vain. With a lifetime of hard work now resting at the head of Tickle Cove Pond, or drifting aimlessly in the sea, many residents packed their meagre belongings and headed to the United States in search of a more prosperous existence.

Brothers Tom and Bill White moved to California, while the majority of those migrating clung to the relative closeness of the Eastern Seaboard.

Many Lane families moved. On July 22, 1922, forty-nine-year-old Charlie Lane went to St. John's and boarded the SS *Rosalind* for New York. Accompanying him were his wife, Elizabeth, thirty-five, and their son, Tom, sixteen. Their eighteen-year-old daughter, Katie, stayed behind with relatives until August 1923. Not long after he and his loved ones had uprooted their lives for what was

Willie John Taylor in a trap skiff unloading a cod trap. A fitting image of life in Tickle Cove since the 1870s. (Courtesy of Mike and Marge O'Shea)

meant to be something better, Charlie was accidentally killed on a Manhattan elevated train.

Other Tickle Cove passengers on that journey included Annie Lane, twenty, Anthony Lane, sixteen, and Agnes

Lane, fourteen. On October 18 that same year, twenty-two-year-old Rosie Lane joined the crowd in the Big Apple.

The following month, on August 31, 1922, eighteen-year-old Mary Lane left Newfoundland on the SS *Silvia* and landed at Ellis Island, New York. Like most Tickle Cove people, she ended up in Massachusetts. While there, she met and married Skipper Jim Duke of Fox Harbour, Placentia Bay.

On November 30, 1922, thirty-six-year-old Arch Skiffington took the train to St. John's, boarded the SS *Rosalind*, and sailed to New York. Everything he worked for in Tickle Cove was gone. Boats, traps, nets, trawls, stores, stages, and wharves: wiped out. He eventually found his way to Boston.

On August 23, 1923, the *Rosalind* carried Charlie Lane's brother Joe to Boston. Along with his wife, Elizabeth, the couple lugged their eight young children. Their daughter, Eileen, eight at the time, left behind her good friends Gertrude Maloney, who was also her cousin, and Annie Kelly. To the shores of America they went, leaving Tickle Cove in the hands of the true survivors, those who stayed.

In addition to the Mohawk Indians, Newfoundlanders are noted for their abilities to work amidst great heights. This put them in demand for the construction of skyscrapers and bridges in the bustling United States. A lifetime at sea provided men with rope-and-pulley skills as well as incredible balance.

From 1929 to 1931, Nick Murphy, father of Tickle Cove

Newfoundlanders taking a well-deserved lunch break on a single steel beam on the frame of the Empire State Building in New York, 800 feet above 6th Avenue. This photo perfectly captures a life far away from the fishery, not to mention the fearlessness of the true Newfoundlander. (Courtesy of Canadian Press Library, September 1932)

descendant Rita Tremlett, worked alongside many Newfoundlanders on the construction of New York's Empire State Building, the tallest building in the world at the time. The amazing photograph of the Newfoundlanders dangling high above Manhattan provides a sense of culture shock Murphy might have experienced at his new job in the United States.

The aftermath of the tidal wave also included a massive migration to other Bonavista Bay communities including Plate Cove, Summerville, Princeton, Sweet Bay, Winter Brook, and Southern Bay. Surnames such as Humby, Gale, and Prince remained absent from the census records of Tickle Cove following 1921.

The harbour was never rebuilt to its former status. Many fishermen built a "make-do,"which is a moveable splitting table on the beach for whatever species was in season at the time. Although people were inevitably sad and lonely, there was little time to brood over their losses. Those who remained continued to pinch a living from the sea as if nothing had happened. Today the tidal wave is just another memory in the few satisfied minds of Tickle Cove old enough to recall the most abrupt change in the history of their town.

10

What Dreams Are Made Of

Every night there'd be someone different in your house. They didn't have to be asked.

Theresa White

MANY PEOPLE BELIEVE in tokens, or signs of death to come. Countless stories have been told of strange events: noises, ghostly sightings, animals acting weirdly, birds falling from the sky, and things going missing. When odd experiences take place, a story's version changes slightly each time it is repeated. If it has a hint of bad in it, a story is guaranteed to appear ten times worse by the time it reaches the end of a community. Regardless of the snowballing effect they produce, tokens always seem to suggest bad luck will occur, mostly death. Belief in tokens, and experiences to support those beliefs, varies from area to area in Newfoundland.

In the absence of modern distractions, ghost stories

provided a wonderful winter pastime. Tickle Cove has made several contributions to the world of the supernatural, involving tokens.

Along the old road to Keels, there is a hole in a cliff once referred to as "Hole in the Wall." Measuring approximately ten feet long, four and a half feet wide, and five feet deep, the cave provided great shelter from nature's elements. Old folks warned not to go in there during a thunderstorm, for "the noise is unbearable."

The following story was told to Captain John Russell by his grandfather Sam, born at Tickle Cove in 1848. The story has been handed down for generations.

THE GHOST OF PHILPOTT'S HOLE

There once lived a fellow in Tickle Cove named Billy Philpott. He was a likeable young man, but he neither feared nor cared for anything on earth. He made lots of fun his own way. He made sad people laugh, and was well-liked by all who knew him.

At the age of twenty-three, he shipped out with six others on the schooner *Mary C* to fish the Labrador. That summer was a very successful one, and they loaded the schooner with fish in no time. Before they were ready to head home, the skipper ordered two men to go ashore and gather enough driftwood to last the trip home. Billy and his buddy were picked to go while the rest of the crew made the schooner ready.

The two men landed on an island a short ways from Bear Cove, where they were anchored all summer. After loading the boat with driftwood, they decided to take a walk around the little island. In doing so, they came to a small graveyard. Eskimo, no doubt, given their knowledge of the area. Soon they found a human skull. Billy says to his buddy, "What a piggin for me boat!" A "piggin" was the common name for a bailer for a small boat.

"You leave that untouched where it is," his buddy said.

"No," said Billy, "I'm taking it home for me boat." His buddy chided him forcefully, but to no avail. Billy was hell-bent on taking it home. Never a word was said about the skull to the other shipmates.

The following fall and winter, Billy used the skull as a piggin in his little boat. When sugar, butter, tea, and flour became scarce around Tickle Cove that winter, Billy decided he would take a walk to King's Cove via Keels Road to get the much-needed necessities. So, off he went, alone.

Figuring he would make the trip in a day, Billy left an hour early. He expected to arrive home not much after dark. On his return, a little while after dark, he arrived at the Hole in the Wall and Rocky Pond Brook. As the brook flowed through the road, a bridge had been built to join the road. When he stepped on the bridge, a dark-faced woman appeared and blew her breath in his face. She then disappeared and never bothered him again . . . at least not for that trip.

He said she stopped him right in his tracks, that he nearly fell down with the fright, but pulled himself together and made it home. Feeling very disturbed, he began to think of what he had done the previous summer. Although he told his frightful experience to everyone, no one believed him.

When spring came again, everything seemed okay. Billy decided he would stay home during the coming summer and fish out of Tickle Cove with hook and line for the herring and caplin sculls, and trawls for the squid cull. Now, this fishery called for lines and trawls, so he decided he would have to go to King's Cove to get them. His fishing buddy said he would go with him, as it would be quite a bundle for one man to bring back. But Billy said, "No, I can handle it. . . . Get the boat ready for painting." And off he went to King's Cove, forgetting all about his ordeal the past winter.

The early spring morning showed a good day and no one expected a snow storm would end the day so tragically. About 3:00 p.m., the snow started to fall, and by four o'clock it worsened as Billy was ready to head home. The shopkeeper tried to persuade him to stay all night. For sure, the storm would be over in the morning. But no, Billy had home on his mind. And home he was going.

When morning came, there was no sign of him at Tickle Cove. After contacting King's Cove and realizing Billy had left at four o'clock the day before, the search began. They went as far as the bridge where Billy had claimed to see the woman, and sure enough there were foot tracks in the snow. At the bridge they backtracked for about a hundred yards and went out into the woods. Not far into the trees, bundles of lines and twine were hanging from a branch. Not much farther on lay Billy's body, partly covered with snow. That was the end of Billy Philpott.

No marks were ever found on his body, indicating he had been molested by man or beast. Some say the Eskimo woman, to whom the skull belonged, was taking out her revenge on Billy that night. More say he may have frightened himself to death when he came to the bridge and thought of his experience the previous winter.

As a result of the tale, Hole in the Wall has been known as Philpott's Hole ever since.

SINGING GHOSTS

When men were launching, hauling, or preparing their boats for a fishing voyage, they sang aloud as they worked. This was heard around the community. The song "Oh, You Jolly Poker" was a familiar sea shanty heard around the Tickle Cove area. One time, following the loss of a boat and her crew in a snowstorm, the song was heard in the air for many years to come by people walking through the town, especially at night.

Two months before Frank Kelly was found dead in Tickle Cove Pond, a strange occurrence took place. Captain John Russell, a close friend of Kelly, remembers all too well that horrible morning in April 1934. What remains strange about Kelly's death is it was forewarned twice, once to someone else, and the second time to himself.

The Funeral on Tickle Cove Pond

It was St. Patrick's Day and the Roman Catholic people of Tickle Cove were preparing for a dance and supper in the school. This denomination believes St. Paddy's Day is exempt from the forty days and forty nights of fasting in Lent, while Protestants believe the opposite.

Joe Quinton was a Protestant from Red Cliff who didn't have a care in the world. He also didn't believe in the religious customs.

One night, he decided to go to a dance. He asked a few of his friends to join him, but they refused, respecting the beliefs instilled in them by their parents. As a result, Joe eventually took off on the snow-covered road from Red Cliff to Tickle Cove by himself. The winter path through Red Cliff Marsh and Tickle Cove Pond was pure ice.

Joe arrived safely in Tickle Cove and was enjoying the entertainment while tickets were sold on a quarter of beef, a sack of potatoes, and a new fifteen-foot punt which someone had built the previous winter. It was worth twenty-five dollars. Although he bought tickets, he didn't win a thing.

After two square dances, supper was served and everyone enjoyed his or her turn at the table. After he finished eating, Joe sat back and watched the dancers. He decided to have one more dance before making ready for home. When leaving, some of his Tickle Cove friends asked him to come over to a house for a drop of home-made brew. "It will make your feet lighter for walking on the ice," one said.

"No thank you," Joe replied, "my feet are light enough tonight. Maybe another time."

Around midnight, Joe was stepping onto the pond to head for home. While walking with his head down to stay warm, Joe looked ahead to watch his step and saw a crowd walking toward him. Rather than turning back, he kept walking along the ice close to the shore. As they drew nearer, Joe saw plenty of room to pass, and some to spare.

When retelling his sighting, Joe said there were eight men in four pairs of two. They had gaffs and rope on their backs. Behind them was a small dog. Not far behind them were eight more men carrying the same items. This was an unusual sight, for there was not a single ice pan in the bay that night. They couldn't be going sealing! Joe took off running, jumping, and skating until he reached the rocky barren separating Red Cliff Marsh from Tickle Cove Pond. When he stopped for a breath, Joe looked back to see nothing but ice and snow on the pond.

More frightened now, Joe ran to Red Cliff. The only lamp burning in the community that night was in the home of his cousin, Mrs. Bertha Quinton, who was waiting for her son, Harry, to return home. Joe made a beeline for the house, opened the door, and fell on the floor. "My God," said Mrs. Quinton, "what's wrong with Joe?" With that, her son arrived home asking the same question.

"He just entered the house as if someone was chasing him, and fell on the floor. His face, white as death," said Bertha.

"Give him a drop of hot brandy, or moonshine," Harry said.

Soon the hot moonshine was poured into Joe's stomach and he started to revive. "Now, Joe," Bertha said, "what's wrong?"

"I met a funeral on Tickle Cove Pond," said Joe.

"You met a few belts of Tickle Cove homemade beer," Bertha laughed. Joe swore he had not taken a drop that night.

Frank Kelly lived in a four-room bungalow with his father, Patrick, and stepmother, Anna, where Tickle Cove's community hall is now located. A month had passed since Joe Quinton's ordeal, and there was still plenty of ice to walk on the pond.

Just after eating his supper, John Russell looked out his window and saw the crippled Frank Kelly struggling up from Johnny Quinton's store in Red Cliff. His food was laid on his hand slide, along with his cane. He was pushing the slide with his good leg, and dragging his crippled leg. Determined to help his friend, Russell readied his family's Newfoundland pony and shouted to Frank he was on his way to help.

He towed Frank and his sled to Tickle Cove by way of the winter path. After arriving at their destination, the men sat and chatted for a while. Frank relayed a dream he had had the night before. "I dreamed I got out of bed last night and I looked out on the pond. I saw a crowd of men with gaffs and ropes on their backs. I wondered where all the men were going with gaffs and ropes. There is not a pan of ice in the bay," he said. In sweat and misery, he woke up and hopped to the window, expecting to see the men on the ice. But there was only an empty cove in front of him.

Frank, feeling a little nervous, did not want John to go home by way of the pond. "The pond is safe enough. We came down over it," said John.

"Makes no difference," said Frank, "you are going home by way of the road," Frank answered. So, to satisfy his friend, John went by road and arrived home feeling very happy about doing a good deed.

Over a breakfast of boiled salt fish, toasted bread, and butter, with his mom and pop, John spoke of Frank's dream and wondered if it had any connection with Joe Quinton's sighting. His mom said, "If I had to remark on things like that from all the bad dreams I've had in my day, no one would be alive in our family." That was the end of that conversation.

After breakfast, John took their pony, Molly, up to a garden in Open Hall. About half way to the meadow the pony halted and jumped to the side of the road, throwing John to the ground, where he landed on his back. With his foot caught in the reins, and the pony obviously disturbed, John fell under Molly's hind leg. Luckily, he was unharmed.

As John sat on a rock by the side of the road, he noticed Mr. Will Barker coming toward him saying, "John, what's wrong with you. Is you sick? You're white as a spirit!"

"No," said John, "I just fell off the pony's back."

"Is you hurt?" asked Mr. Barker. Upon learning John was okay, Mr. Barker continued on his way to Red Cliff. John got to the pasture, put Molly in, and headed back for home.

As he approached the first houses going into Red Cliff from Open Hall, John saw three women standing in the middle of the road. They appeared excited and were talking aloud. When he reached them, one of the women said, "My dear, John, there's awful bad news."

"What's that?" asked John.

"Frank Kelly just drowned in Tickle Cove Pond," she said.

"Not Frank," he said. "It can't be true."

"Joe Lane just called Mrs. Lizzie on the phone and told her," she said, "The whole place is in an uproar and no one hardly knows what they are doing."

"He also said a crowd of men are gone on the pond where he fell in and are dragging for his body," said another lady.

The home of Theresa (Legge) White. This silent witness to the funeral on Tickle Cove Pond has stood for almost 150 years. (Author photo)

The news was sure to kill poor old Uncle Paddy, as Frank was his only child. When Joe Lane called back with an update for Mrs. Lizzie, he said Frank had seen his Uncle Con Kelly on the other side of the pond cutting small trees and putting them on his slide. After a little while, Frank made his way to his uncle. When he reached Con, he said, "This [wood] is awful small, too small to cut. I'm going over to the other side. It's bigger there." So away he went, not looking where he was going. He went too close to the brook where the ice was thin, and before he knew anything, he was gone headfirst into the water. Uncle Con witnessed this and started to roar, running toward Tickle Cove for help. But it was too late. Frank was gone.

Con Kelly lived for some years after the incident, but was never heard to speak louder than a whisper. His vocal cords were damaged in his effort to save his nephew.

The men from Tickle Cove soon had a boat up the brook, and with gaffs and other gear and they found Frank's body and slide. There was only about five feet of water in the brook. The boat was placed on the slide.

With the body in the boat, eight men in four groups of two pulled the load with rope, while another eight men got behind and pushed.

Out of sadness, John Russell did not attend the wake of his friend. He opted to go to the funeral Mass in Open Hall instead.

11

A Community's Finest Resource: Captain John Russell

Take care of yourself in your young days. In your middle age, respect your family and give them your full support in thought, word, and deed. For sure, they will always respect you. I've found that out in my long-lived life.

Captain John Russell (age 100)

KNOWLEDGE IS THE key which gives substance to all facets of life. This gift is not divine. It is best obtained from experience. Though he only spent the first week of his life in Tickle Cove, Captain John Russell is, by far, the community's greatest source of knowledge. His story is one of true grit and determination to make the best of a not-so-easy world.

John Russell was born at midnight, December 10, 1906. Consequently, he celebrates his birthday on December 11. Just a few days after his birth, his mother, twenty-year-old Ida Jane Russell, contracted pneumonia while washing clothes. She passed away a short time later. It was her wish, should anything happen to her, that John be cared for by her sister, Beatrice Oldford, in Red Cliff. And that is what happened.

Russell's father, Fred, soon left to find employment in the United States. Fred worked for fifty years with the Boston/Maine Railway. He died at the age of eighty-nine and is buried in Massachusetts. Attaining grand ages is not uncommon for the Russells of Tickle Cove. John's grandfather, Sam Russell, also lived well into his nineties.

Although he grew up next door in Red Cliff, John always considered Tickle Cove home. In his childhood days, he would "take off running" to his Uncle Harold Wilson's in Tickle Cove when school at Red Cliff was over. In his book, *Memories of a Lifetime*, he recounts highlights of his life from birth to his last days in the woods at age seventy-seven. Russell left Red Cliff and moved to Bonavista in 1952, but still took time on Sundays to drive his family to the place he will always called home, something he still does today.

The captain's experiences could easily fill a hundred history books. Not only do we get facts from his tales, we vicariously experience feelings through his intense method of storytelling. He puts you right there. There's no magic, just honesty. Call it what you will; it's good for all which ails you.

Russell experienced every aspect of Newfoundland's

fishing and sealing history. After a stint as skipper of his own schooner, *Flora MacIvor*, he decided there were better ways to make a living. Better ways, however, did not mean easier ways. From teaching school at Tickle Cove to lugging cement in the early 1920s at Humbermouth, Russell always kept his head up for the next best thing.

In April 1927, he boarded the SS *Far North* and headed to the United States where he stayed for six years. Now twenty-one years of age, and reunited with his father, he too worked on the Boston/Maine Railway. The Russells kept in close contact with their old acquaintances, the McCormacks and the Walkers from Tickle Cove. Captain Russell is the only person living who partied with Mark Walker, a story in itself.

During those six years in the United States, he went back to Red Cliff and convinced the love of his life to marry him, and together they went back to Massachusetts. In a short time, his wife contracted tuberculosis, soon enticing them to return home again. While keeping up with the struggle of daily survival, Russell watched helplessly as his first love fell victim to the disease and died. Heartbroken, he carried on. Not many years later, accepting God's will, he bounced back and married a beautiful girl from Port Rexton, Trinity Bay North. Together they had six children. Today they have seventeen grandchildren and eight great-grandchildren.

Russell worked for Sir William Coaker, and studied navigation with Captain Abram Kean. He was seasoned by the salt of the sea while working with several Newfoundland Railway coastal steamers, as well as a year on the *Flora MacIvor*. Russell played a vital role during the Second World War as skipper of the Royal Canadian Navy tug *Cachalot*, towing targets in the enemy line and delivering supplies for the Boom Defense at Wabana, Bell Island. It was during this period the Germans torpedoed four Allied battleships. "You didn't know what time he [the enemy] was gonna come up and point a gun at you and let go, you know. One shell blows the hell out of the water for miles," he said.

Following the war, Russell found himself engaged wholeheartedly in lumber and mill production, as well as the lobster business. In addition, he spent five seasons as manager of Fishery Products International's (FPI) fishing stations on the Labrador coast. Following his retirement from fishing, Russell skippered the yacht of successful businessman Chester Dawe for three years, bringing Dawe and his friends on trouting excursions to Labrador.

This man is not all work. He is also an accomplished songwriter, musician, poet, and singer. Russell penned his first song at the age of thirty-nine. Since then he has artistically commented on many topics which demonstrate first-hand familiarity with ways once reflected in our proud and rugged heritage. Russell's book, *Memories of a Lifetime*, was published when he was ninety-one years of age. His humorous contribution to provincial government happenings of 2003, *The Election Song*, won the hearts and minds of people far and wide.

Darrell Duke

The style in which Russell presents his words provides a drop of soul maintenance and leaves one yearning for a taste of more. He is in constant demand by writers and researchers, all soliciting for a sliver of his time.

The following two songs are examples of Captain John Russell's brilliance with the pen and his boundless devotion to the cornerstones of our past:

Captain John Russell was born at Tickle Cove in 1906. He lives in Bonavista with his wife, Gwen. (Author photo)

146

GOOD OLD "WATERLOO"

The wind was cold, it snowed like mad, my feet were frozen stiff.
I fought my way up to the road,' twas in my mind to quit.
But a voice from out of somewhere said don't feel too blue,
For back out home, not far from here, is a good old Waterloo.

Napoleon was a warrior, and a good one I declare,
Although he lost the battle in the Waterloo affair.
He was always claimed a hero, a man of high renown
Which caused his claret blood to flow upon the battleground.

Now the Waterloo that I know best is a good old-fashioned stove,
A box-like oven with two doors, and a six-inch pipe above.
With junks of spruce and likewise birch, one never saw the like,
The heat that came from that old stove on a frosty, stormy night.

But let me take you back awhile, to the place where I was born,
Down by the pond in Tickle Cove, on a cold and snowy morn.
When Father got the call to arms, the first thing he did do,
Was fill up the stove, then light a fire, in the good old Waterloo.

There are other makes, I can't forget, their names I can recall,
The Standard and the Comfort tried hard to beat them all.
Try how they liked, they always lost, and nothing they could do,
In making beans for breakfast, like the good old Waterloo.

When it was time for dinner, and the pot was full of food,

With cabbage and potatoes, and everything that's good.
And Mom would ask the blessing, the next thing she would do,
Was poke a birch junk in the stove, the good old Waterloo.

We would all sit down and eat our meal made by our Mother's hand.
The old-time white sail pudding, covered in with jam.
We loved our old-time cooking, especially rabbit stew,
Fish and brewis, and seal fat cakes, cooked on the Waterloo.

Now all good times are past and gone, likewise my Mother, too,
Electric stoves and oil pushed out the Waterloo.
But if I had one request to make, I would ask my God to do—
Give me one good frosty night, with my good old Waterloo.

GRANDFATHER'S BARREL ROCKING CHAIR

Grandfather was a fisherman, he lived in T & C,
He always made his living on the land and from the sea.
When his day's work was over, he would always like to share,
A little bit of humour in his barrel rocking chair.

Then early in the morning, he was always up and gone.
Out with his other brothers to the far-off fishing grounds.
Those days there were no engines, no help in any way,
Only sails and paddles were the order of the day.

From spring 'til fall he toiled on, and never did complain,
He met the days and months and years, no matter how they came.

But always in the twilight hours, if he had time to spare,
He always had a little nod in his barrel rocking chair.

But early in his married life, when he was young and strong,
God took from him my grandma, and left him there to mourn.
For she was only forty-five, just in the prime of life,
Grandpa was only forty-eight when he lost his loving wife.

Now after days of mourning, a new life he put on,
He moved away from Tickle Cove, and with his oldest son,
He made his home in Southern Bay, but still had time to spare,
To have a little rest each day in his barrel rocking chair.

Then after three long years or more, again he changed his life,
He settled down again once more, and took another wife.
But always in the evening hours, when it was bright and clear,
He loved to sing those dear old hymns, sitting in his barrel chair.

The last time that I saw him, his age was ninety-three.
He just sat down to take a rest, and have a cup of tea.
And Grandma Two was with him, to him she was sincere.
For she always liked to see him rest in his barrel rocking chair.

And now they both are gone to rest, their wishes are fulfilled,
He lies to rest in Southern Bay, and she in Summerville.
The dearest things they left behind, they both found time to spare,
Hers the Holy Bible, his the barrel chair.

Appendix

TICKLE COVE by Eileen O'Shea (1977)

There is a place seemingly far from others,
An undernourished amount of progress,
Nature still dominates.

Horses and cows wander free,
Man-made luxuries hard to come by,
The sky is a puzzle,
its stars brightly shining.

Sunsets pink, purple, orange, and yellow,
Open doors, hearts kind,
Rarely mean and unfriendly.

The warmth is a drink shared,
And drunk with others,
Time passes quickly,
Its ticking appreciated as company.

Impressions are vivid,
A little hard for words to describe,
Tickle Cove, the name of such a place,
Is the keeper of my poem.

Appendix

Flair of pen or imagination,
Could never do justice to this—
God-given beauty.

FROM THE BIG HILL
by Darrell Duke

A stranger to your toughness and beauty,
Marvelling above your famous pond,
Ripples of days long ago trickle through the buzz of a saw,
Longers peek over rocks and across the water to Old Gerald's Hill,
Multicoloured stone, hand-painted by its Creator,
Fallen to land once laden with berry pickers galore,
Tuckamore cautiously push the past aside,
Securing themselves a place in your tomorrow,
A multiple blue-grey sky casts a seasonable backdrop,
For gulls en route to nowhere,
An old Enterprise lies bottom-up;
Evidence of a home no more—
Where winter mitts were placed to dry;
Where water, carried on strong backs from the pond,
Boiled in waiting; where scalding tea steamed,
In pursuit of hard bread,
Overflowing cups. Slurped from saucers;
Cast-iron pots clanking their covers for stew and doughballs;
Boiled salt fish; potatoes from the Pond Gardens,
Aprons and oilskins hung in the warmth,
Of splits, junks, and moose soup,

Scents of life's hard work as fresh as the hare hung in the pantry,
Dough rising under the blanket,
Painted-shut windows given a bang and raised;
Storm door tied to a nail;
Cooling the kitchen at the height of a time,
A song and a story about the day's events. The daybed full,
Planks, glistening of pot liquor and freshly swept sand,
Buckling under feet driven by moonshine and fiddles;
Set back in place by the spring thaw,
Things were made to last in those days,
Surrounded by more than physical beauty;
Intrigued by a feeling of warmth,
Through an end-of-August breeze,
There is something beautiful here.

The outhouse. Before modern plumbing, and where the *Family Fireside* was used for more than just reading. (Author photo)

Sources

1. Department of Government Services and Lands, Surveys and Mapping Division.

2. *Ships and Seafarers of Atlantic Canada*, CD-Rom, Memorial University of Newfoundland, 1998.

3. American Family Immigration History Center, Ellis Island, New York.

4. Census Records, Statistics Canada.

5. Lovell's 1871 Directory.

6. McAlpine's Directories (1894–97, 1898, 1904).

7. *Dictionary of Newfoundland English*, Second Edition, Toronto: University of Toronto Press, 1990.

8. "Saved by a Dream" (Robert Parsons, from *Sea Dogs & Skippers*, Garry Cranford, Flanker Press, 2001).

9. Long, James E. *The Hard and the Aisey*. St. John's, NL: ESP Press, 1998.

10. "Restart of the Races on Tickle Cove Pond," *The Packet*.

11. *Newfoundland Will Books.* (Judy Benson, A Collection of Newfoundland Wills).

12. http://irishgenealogy.com. (Robert Pelosi, www.mullowney.com).

13. Covenstead. (diviningrods.msnw).

14. http://ngb.chebucto.org.

15. A. C. Hunter Library, St. John's (Newfoundland Collection).

16. Gordon King (photographs).

17. King's Cove Church Records (RC).

18. Shirley Foley (Maloney Family History).

19. Smith, Cecil Woodham. *The Great Hunger*, Hamish Hamilton Ltd., 1962.

20. Feltham, Jack. *The Islands of Bonavista Bay*. St. John's, NL: Harry Cuff, 1986.

21. Canadian Press Library.

22. Hutchinson's Directory (1864-65).

23. Newfoundland's Grand Banks' Genealogical and Historical Data.

24. The *Evening Telegram*.

25. The *Daily News*.

26. Herman Russell.

27. Newfoundland Archives (Colonial Building, St. John's).

28. CBC Cod Time Line (Online Report).

29. Destination Newfoundland and Labrador.

30. Industry Canada (Community Demographics).

31. *Encyclopedia of Newfoundland and Labrador.* Cuff, R. H., 1993.

32. *Decks Awash* (March–April, 1984) Vol. 13, No. 2.

33. Newfoundland Genweb Data (Bonavista Bay Fishing Rooms 1805).

34. Roberts, Danny. *The Greenland Disaster of 1898.*

35. Harrington, Michael. *Prime Ministers of Newfoundland.* Cuff, R. H. 1991.

36. Harris, Michael. *Lament for an Ocean.*

37. http://ngb.chebucto.org/Newspaper-Obits/lindex-old-news.shtml.

38. PC Newfoundland and Labrador (news release May 14, 2003).

39. Chaulk Murray, Hilda. *More Than 50%.* Breakwater Books, 1979.

40. 'Tropical Traditions' (www.tropicaltraditions.com/codliveroil.htm).

41. Dr. Philip Hiscock.

42. Memorial University of Newfoundland Folklore Archives.

43. The *Evening Advocate* (October 1921 Storm News).

44. Leith Quinton (1972 Interview with Mr. Fred Oldford).

45. Major, Kevin. *As Near to Heaven by Sea.* Penguin Books, 2001.

46. *Wall Street Journal* (Newfoundlanders Working in the US).

47. www.pigeoninlet.com (Newfoundland Folk Songs).

48. *Community and Process* (Gerald Thomas/J.D.A. Widdowson, Editors, Breakwater, 1991).

49. Colony of Avalon Glossary.

50. Russell, Captain John. *Memories of a Lifetime.* ESP Press, 1998.

Acknowledgements

For inviting a stranger into your lives and kindly offering countless mug-ups and intriguing conversation, for the feelings, knowledge, and photographs comprising this book, thank you:

Captain John Russell and wife, Gwen
Gertrude Maloney
Gerald and Hilda Quinton
Mary Mullowney
Theresa White
Rita Tremblett
Annie and Mary Kelly
Ron and Jesse Fitzgerald
Jim and Carrie Oldford
Gerard and Mary Lou Maloney
Martha Fitzgerald
Jim Lane
Mike and Marge O'Shea
Albert and Molly Legge
Mark Kelly
Gus Quinton
Gordon King

About the Author

Darrell Duke was born in Placentia, Newfoundland, in 1970, and dedicates his life to music and to the preservation of his province's cultural heritage. He is an accomplished musician, playwright, poet, journalist, singer, and songwriter. Darrell's book of poetry, *If You Look Closely, You'll See* was published in 1999. His self-titled debut music CD was released in 2006. He is currently writing a novel based on events of the 1927 August Gale in Placentia Bay.

Index

Index

Index

Newfoundland railway coastal boats 25
Nimoy, Leonard 117
Nimrod 62
Noggin Cove, Notre Dame Bay 41–42

O'Neil, Catherine 7
O'Reilly, Cyril v
O'Shea x
O'Shea, Eileen 150
O'Shea, Marge x, 52, 122, 126, 155
O'Shea, Mike x, 52, 122, 126, 155
Oh, You Jolly Poker 134
Oldford, Beatrice 143
Oldford, Fred 100, 124
Oldford, Gus 100
Oldford, Jim 19, 42, 100, 155
Oldford, Kim 155
Oldford, Lloyd 117
Oldford, Rex 80
Oldford, William 112–113
Open Hall viii, xii, 2, 13–14, 16–18, 25, 28–30, 59, 74, 78–80, 100, 107–108, 138–139, 141
Over 8–9, 13
Over, Gladys 19
Over, Henry 7–8
Over, John 19
Over, Nellie 19
Ovier 8–9

Pearl 39
Pelican 42
Phillips, Patricia 116–117
Philpott 9
Philpott, Billy 131, 134
Philpott, Walter 73
Philpott's Hole 131–134
Pittman 108
Pittman, Gwendolyn 19
Plate Cove 2, 17, 25–26, 42, 66, 73, 80, 108, 111, 129
Pond Gardens xii, 99, 103, 152
Port Rexton 144
Powell 8
Prang, Louis 95
Prince 129
Prince Alfred 24–25
Prince, Alfred 28
Prince Edward Island 75
Prince, George 39, 41
Prince, Jack 25
Prince of Wales 24
Prince, Robert 69
Prince, Sam 101
Princeton 2, 25–28, 60, 77, 129
Protestant 12, 15, 86, 135

Quinton 28, 42, 55, 72, 75–78, 80, 84
Quinton, Andrew 72

Quinton, Bertha 134–135
Quinton, Dick 102
Quinton, Dolf 82, 84
Quinton, Gerald 77, 82, 84, 106, 108, 118, 155
Quinton, Gus 155
Quinton, Hilda 155
Quinton, Jessie 19
Quinton, Joe 133, 137–138
Quinton, John 72–73, 75–76, 78, 84, 89, 125, 137
Quinton, Oldford
Quinton, William Sr. 59, 72–73, 82

Randell, Gus 100
Random Sound 41
Red Cliff viii, xii, 2, 13, 16, 19, 25, 28–29, 42, 55, 59–60, 75–76, 78–80, 100, 102, 107, 113, 117, 124–125, 135–137, 139, 143–144
Red Cliff Island 72, 118
Red Cliff Marsh 135
Rocky Pond 98
Rocky Pond Brook 132
Roe 8
Rolls 9
Rooney, Mickey 117
SS *Rosalind* 125, 127
Russell 9, 13, 124, 143–144

161